CONTENTS

KU-650-166

So you know...   **4**
    Starting Word 2007   5
    Finding your way around   6
    Final check and save   7

Task 1   **On form**   **10**
    Planning your document   14
    Checkpoint   39
    Assessment point   39
    Get ahead   39

Task 2   **Putting it together**   **40**
    Formatting the form   44
    Hyperlinks   54
    Checkpoint   57
    Assessment point   57
    Get ahead   57

Task 3   **A brilliant report**   **58**
    Choose a template   61
    The template layout   62
    Checkpoint   87
    Assessment point   87
    Get ahead   87

The Project   **Check your performance**   **88**
    Some tips   89
    Resources   90
    Advice   90
    Assessment point   94

Index   **95**

This book is about learning to use the Microsoft Office application Word 2007. Word 2007 makes your computer into a 'Word processor', which is one of the most common ways in which computers are used in schools and businesses. The letters that get sent from your school will be produced on a word processor. Books and newspaper articles will all have started as word processed documents, and no doubt you will be typing a few essays on a word processor! The most common documents used by businesses are letters, faxes and reports.

All of these documents will contain mainly words that will be styled using things like different fonts and text sizes, bullet points, bold or italic letters and aligning the text on one or other side of the page (see page 6 to see where you would find all of these styling or formatting tools). A word-processing software program like Word is the best choice of software for any document that contains mainly words.

However, Word can do much more than format words. There are many skills that you will be learning about in your studies – such as the need to save your work appropriately, display data in different ways such as text, tables, graphs and images, write documents suitable for your audience and their purpose, review and refine your work, write a good questionnaire and collect the right data, and share information digitally – and this book will show you how you can use the program Word to help you to present all of this kind of information.

The skills that you will learn are:

Task 1: How to create a form to help with collecting data.
Task 2: How to insert and edit text and images, and include hyperlinks in your documents.
Task 3: How to use templates, insert tables and graphs, format text and use WordArt.

You can use this book by working through from Task 1 to Task 3 or you can download the finished files that have been produced in Task 1 and work on those in Task 2. For instance, if you don't want to create an interactive form, download the finished form and use it in Task 2 to learn how to change text and images. Or you can start with Task 3 if those are the skills that you want to learn first. It's up to you…

So, much of this book is about using a word-processing program to reduce the amount of work that you need to do; that has to be good!

This book also helps you to develop your Functional Skills in ICT. This is all about you being able to use your skills in the way that best suits the activity that you have been given – in other words, *why* you are doing something in the way that you have chosen. For example, you always need to be thinking about the purpose of what you are doing – what has it got to do with the task, what kind of impact do you want to achieve, who is going to see or use what you're working on, i.e. who is your audience, and what is the background of the situation – for example, do you need to produce a formal or informal document? By considering all of these things you should be able to produce the right kind of documents that are 'fit for purpose', i.e. they do the job they need to do. A lot to take in at once I know, but have a look at the Functional Skills tabs as you work through the book and they'll show you what all this means in practice … so that you can use them to help you with your project.

Once you have completed the three Tasks, you are going to use the skills that you have learnt to reduce the workload for someone else. You are going to create a document that can be used for sports day entries, along with an advert that can be used to advertise the event. You will need to devise a simple way for entrants to record their scores in track and field events.

Before you start it is best to have a look around Word 2007, because the way it works and its appearance on the screen is sometimes different to that of other word processors.

STARTING WORD 2007

Either:

1. Click on **Start**.

2. Click **All Programs**.

3. Select **Microsoft Office 2007**.

4. Select **Microsoft Office Word 2007**.

Figure Intro.1

Or just double click the **Microsoft Office Word 2007** icon on the desktop:

FINDING YOUR WAY AROUND

You have probably used word processors many times before, but it is best to read this section through and do the exercise because there are some new alternative ways of working in Word 2007 of which you need to be aware.

Once Word 2007 has loaded, you will see a screen very like that in Figure Intro.2.

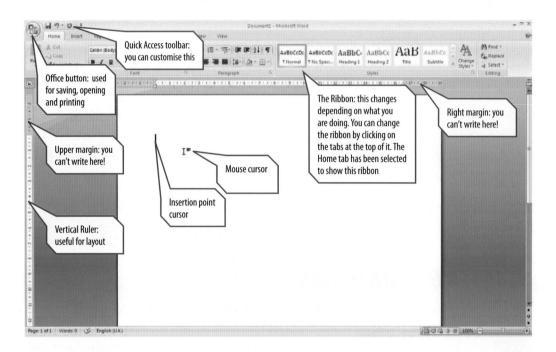

Figure intro.2

Here is a list of what the tabs and ribbons that you'll use do. The words in italic are the main skills you'll use on that ribbon.

Tab	You will find the following tools on the ribbon:
Home	Clipboard, Font, Paragraph, Styles, Editing *Formatting tools and Find and Replace*
Insert	Pages, Tables, Illustrations, Links, Header & Footer, Text, Symbols *Textboxes, Word Art, Date, Hyperlinks, Table*
Page Layout	Themes, Page Setup, Page Background, Paragraph, Arrange *Page orientation, Watermark, Line spacing*
View	Document views, Show/Hide, Zoom, Window, Macros *Zoom*
Design	Table Style Options, Table Styles, Draw Borders *Table Borders and shading*
Layout	Table, Row & Columns, Merge, Cell Size, Alignment, Data *Adding and deleting Rows & Columns*

Figure Intro.3 shows the main tools you'll use for formatting your text.

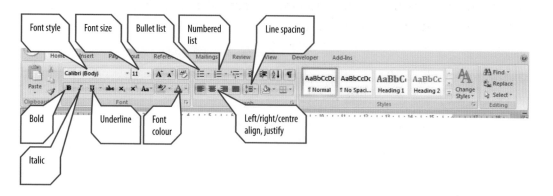

Figure Intro.3

FINAL CHECK AND SAVE

Word is the software that you would choose if you are writing documents that include mainly text (rather than images or other types of information) so it is important that you are able to check your spelling quickly and easily as our documents may be very long, because poor spelling in a document makes a bad impression.

Word puts a wavy red line under a word that is spelt incorrectly or a word that it doesn't recognise. By right clicking on the word, the software will either give you a list of alternative words that you can choose from or if it just doesn't recognise the word but you know it is correct, you can click on Ignore. If you want to check your whole document from the start, you can instruct Word to search for all of the misspelt words. Click on the **Review** tab and then on **Spelling and Grammar** in the **Proofing** section and choose the correct word from the list, or ignore it.

Saving files

> ### TIP
> *It's useful to include the Save As icon on the Quick Access toolbar. Click on the Office button (see Figure Intro.3) and right click on the Save As icon in the drop-down menu. Select Add to Quick Access Toolbar; this will add the Save As icon to the Quick Access Toolbar, which makes it more accessible when you are working.*

  Click the Office button and select **Save As**.

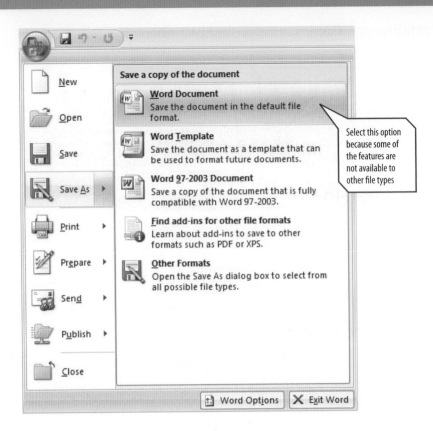

Figure Intro.4

You have a number of choices – see Figure Intro.4.

 Click your choice (it's best to use the **Word Document** file type).

The **Save As** dialogue box appears:

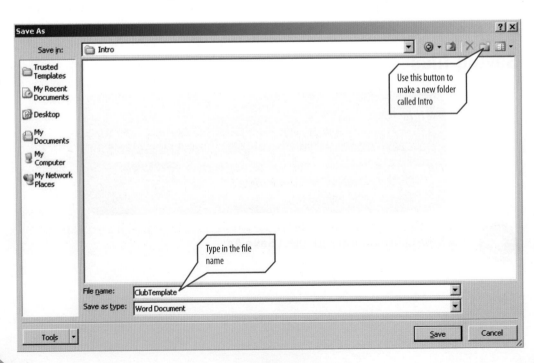

Figure intro.5

It is good practice to save all of the files for a project in their own folder so you don't confuse files.

Printing files

 Click on the Office button, select **Print** and then click **Print Preview**:

Figure intro.6

In Print Preview you can get an idea of what the whole page looks like. Then to print your work select the **Print** option.

ON FORM

TASK BRIEF

The Head of Year 7
has sent you this email . . .

BACKGROUND

You are going to create a form. Forms are very often used to collect information or to help people register for services such as when booking a hotel, where the names and numbers of guests staying and the dates of the holiday would be recorded on the form. As we are using a computer and not paper, we can make one form that can be re-used by several people. Each person using the form will leave their details and these will be held on the computer.

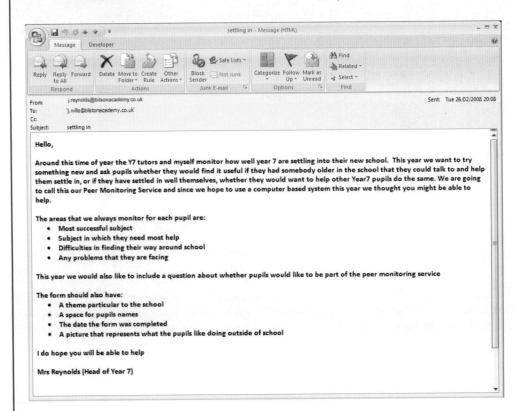

Figure 1.1

The email shown in Figure 1.1 contains the following text:

Hello,

Around this time of year the Y7 tutors and myself monitor how well year 7 are settling into their new school. This year we want to try something new and ask pupils whether they would find it useful if they had somebody older in the school that they could talk to and help them settle in, or if they have settled in well themselves, whether they would want to help other Year7 pupils do the same. We are going to call this our Peer Monitoring Service and since we hope to use a computer based system this year we thought you might be able to help.

The areas that we always monitor for each pupil are:
- Most successful subject
- Subject in which they need most help
- Difficulties in finding their way around school
- Any problems that they are facing

This year we would also like to include a question about whether pupils would like to be part of the peer monitoring service

The form should also have:
- A theme particular to the school
- A space for pupils names
- The date the form was completed
- A picture that represents what the pupils like doing outside of school

I do hope you will be able to help

Mrs Reynolds (Head of Year 7)

SOFTWARE SKILLS

You will learn how to:

> Organise your work using folders and filenames

> Use a picture as a watermark

> Change a style

> Add content controls

> Change the way content controls work using Properties

FUNCTIONAL SKILLS

As you work through this task the Functional Skills tabs will explain to you why the task tackles this brief in the way shown here and explain why you would choose to:

> Plan your work

> Match font and document styles with the audience

> Test work

CAPABILITY

You will be demonstrating capability in planning your document for your audience.

VOCABULARY

You should learn these new words and understand what they mean:

> Form

> Layout

> Style

> Control

> Rich text

> Drop-down list

> Properties

RESOURCES

There are 2 files for this task:

background_school.jpg

IntroText.docx

The file MonitoringLayout.docm is the finished form – use this to show you what you are aiming to produce.

The file Layout.docx can be used to help you plan your form

You can download these files from www.payne-gallway.co.uk

TARGET POINT

Turn the page to see your Target Points for this task.

Level 3	Level 4	Level 5	Level 6
You have saved a file as MonitoringLayout in the Monitoring folder	You have saved the appropriate files in the folder called Monitoring		
You have located and opened the correct image file for the task	You have developed a plan for your form		
You have followed the instructions to insert tabs	You have changed the tabs to suit your plan	You can say why you have used the tab stops	
You have followed the instructions to insert a control box	You have changed the control box to suit your plan	You can say why you have used the controls	
	You have selected a suitable image for your form	You have designed a method suitable for collecting data from a large number of people	You can say why the form would help to collect the data on the monitoring system
	You have changed the form and added controls with different options to choose from	You have changed the form and added controls with options that are suitable for your purpose	
	You have tested that your form works		

SOFTWARE SKILLS

Undoing and redoing an action

OK, let's make a start.

It is very important to choose the correct software for a task because using the correct software can make working much easier. In this case the finished document is largely text, so word-processing software is a suitable choice.

Task 1 is about creating a form that can be used to collect data about the views of students and how they're getting on at school. We want this form to be quick and easy for the students to fill in so we're going to help them out by creating an interactive form where they can choose their answers from a list of options. Remember this task is about showing you how to create a data collection form so that when you create your own questionnaires and write questions that you want to know the answers to, you can use these techniques to help you build the form to collect the answers. You can then email this type of form to users for them to fill in and email back.

But before we start, there are two very important buttons you need to know about – they're called Undo and Redo. You'll find them both on the Quick Access Toolbar.

This button means that you don't need to worry too much about making a mistake – as long as you don't save your document before you press it! If you make a change to your document that is not right, you can click this button to 'undo' your change.

This button lets you put back the change you have just undone. When there are no undone changes to put back, it looks like this and lets you repeat your last action.

TARGET POINT

Have a look at the following statements before you start your task so that you know what you are aiming for.

Although you will not make your own decisions on the design of the form in Task 1, you can use what you learn here to help with other work that will be awarded a particular level.

Organising your work

Before you start any task you should organise the area of the computer where you are going to save the work.

 Load Word 2007 and make a new folder called Monitoring.

 Save a new file called MonitoringLayout in your new folder (save the file as a Word document):

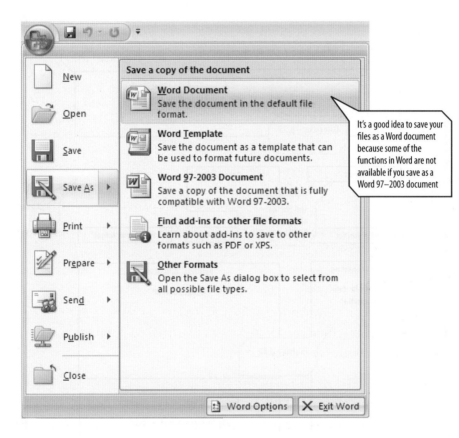

Figure 1.2

Navigate to the folder containing the file:

background_school.jpg

and save the picture file in the Monitoring folder so that you have your own copy to hand when needed.

SOFTWARE SKILLS
Creating new folders and files

SOFTWARE SKILLS
Navigating to find a file

FUNCTIONAL SKILLS
Organising your files and folder structure – you should keep your folders organised so that you can keep your work for each project stored separately. You should store your files using suitable names so that you can find an individual file easily

PLANNING YOUR DOCUMENT

Here is an example of a plan for our form. You can see that we have left space for everything that Mrs Reynolds has asked. You can work through the whole of Task 1 to see how you would build this form exactly or you could plan your own form. If you want to plan your own form, use the callouts below to decide which type of controls you want to add to your form.

FUNCTIONAL SKILLS

Plans are important because:

- *They show all of your ideas so you could easily present them to your client (Mrs Reynolds) and they are easy and cheap to change if your client doesn't like them*

- *When the project is under way, you can keep looking back at the documents to make sure you have done everything you needed to*

FUNCTIONAL SKILLS

Drawing your layout as shown in Figure 1.3 enables you to work out how to fit all of the information into the space you have in a way that is clear and easy for your user to understand

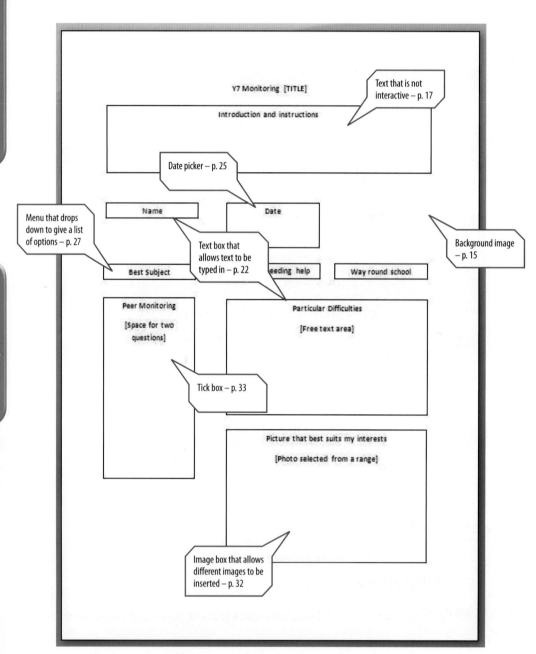

Figure 1.3

Background

The email from Mrs Reynolds asks you to make the form with a theme related to the school. We are going to do this by taking a picture of part of the school and making it into the 'watermark' on the form.

A watermark is another way of making a faint background, and is useful because it means any text you put on top of it can be easily read.

SOFTWARE SKILLS
Adding a watermark

 Click on the **Page Layout** tab.

 Click the **Watermark** button in the **Page Background** group.

The drop-down box contains a number of standard options, but we want to choose the picture of the school, so…

 Select **Custom Watermark** (towards the bottom of the drop-down box).

The **Printed Watermark** dialogue box loads:

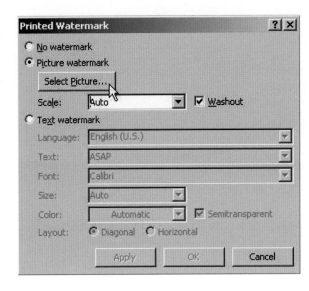

Figure 1.4

FUNCTIONAL SKILLS

Choosing images – always ensure you know who the owner of the image is (we call them the copyright holder) as you may need to seek their permission to use it. You should match the style of image to your document and audience. We are producing a 'formal' document so the image we have chosen is an official photograph of the school

Click **Select Picture**.

 Navigate to the picture of the school (background_school) in your Monitoring folder.

 Double click the file.

The picture appears over the blank page of the Word file as a faint image.

www.edinburgharchitecture.co.uk
Figure 1.5

That's all there is to it – simple. Now let's consider the text we need to add to the page.

Adding a title

The title needs to be horizontal in the centre of the page:

 Centre the insertion point cursor (**Home** tab, **Paragraph** group).

 Type in the title 'Year 7 Monitoring Form'.

Hmm – it doesn't have much impact, does it?

We'll change the formatting of the title later once we have the other objects in place on the form, but we will need to remember to leave sufficient space on the page for the larger size of the title.

There is another problem here: the title is above the watermark. It would look better lower down so that it is over the watermark.

 Click at the beginning of the title and press **Enter**; this will move the title down one line. It is now on top of the watermark:

Year 7 Monitoring Form

Figure 1.6

Now we need to give the users some instructions on how to use the form.

Click the **Insert** tab and then click the **Shapes** button in the **Illustrations** group.

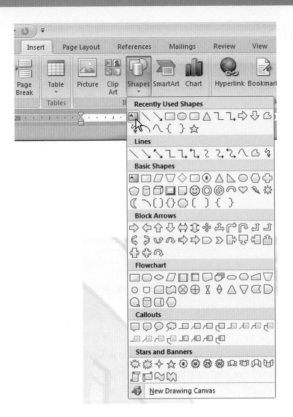

Figure 1.7

The mouse pointer changes into a cross. $+$

Draw the box by clicking and dragging. Make the box about 125 mm wide and 55 mm deep.

You can judge the size of the box using the Ruler.

> **TIP**
>
> *If your Ruler does not measure in mm, it is easy to change it.*
>
> *Click on the Office button and then select Word Options. In the Word Options dialogue box, select Advanced and then scroll down to Display. You will see the 'Show measurement in units of' settings, which you just set to mm and click OK.*

 12   Now navigate to your Monitoring folder and open the file

IntroText.

FUNCTIONAL SKILLS

Text boxes – by using a text box we can change the information in it without affecting anything else on the page and it means we can move it about the page easily

SOFTWARE SKILLS

Using keyboard shortcuts to copy and paste

 13   Select all of the text, then hold down the **Ctrl** key on your keyboard.   Ctrl

 14   Now press the **C** key.

That's done the copying; now for the pasting!

 15 Close the IntroText file.

 16 Click in the text box that you have just made on your form.

 17 Hold down the **Ctrl** key again and then press the **V** key.

Magic!

Inserting controls

You are going to make a form that will be suitable for any of the Year 7 users to fill in. To do this you are going to place special objects called 'controls' on the form.

These 'controls' will make the form interactive so that users can simply choose their answers from a list of options. This means that Mrs Reynolds will get the exact information that she is looking for. The form can then be emailed to each pupil and emailed back when completed, making it much less time consuming for Mrs Reynolds than handing out the forms on paper.

First of all you need to move the insertion point cursor (look back at Figure intro.3). It needs to be under the text box.

FUNCTIONAL SKILLS

When you create these forms you need to think carefully about the type of questions you want to ask and make sure that you choose the correct 'control'. For example, if you want somebody to be able to give any answer because you've asked an open question, you would choose a control that lets them add any text, but if you asked a closed question that had a Yes/No answer, you might choose a tick box control

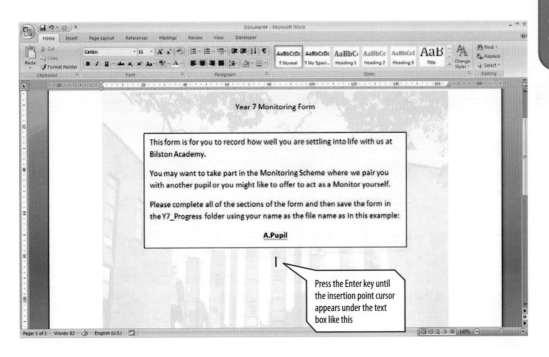

Figure 1.8

 18 Press the **Enter** key about 8 times to move the insertion point cursor under the text box.

Look back at Figure 1.3 on page 14. Most of the layout splits the page vertically into three columns. Look at the row of text boxes – 'Best Subject', etc.

We are going to place our controls at these points across the page. Let's look at how you set them.

Setting tabs

Click in the **tab toolbox**, which is found where the vertical and horizontal rulers meet:

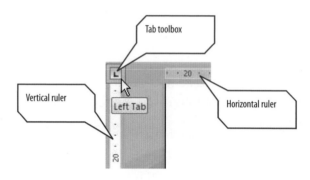

Figure 1.9

 Click until you see the L shape as in Figure 1.9.

We need three tab stops to help us to line up the controls across the page; have a look at this:

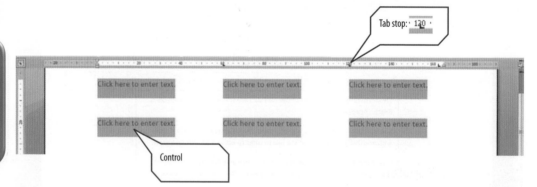

Figure 1.10

You can see that the left side of the controls line up with a tab stop.

To make the tab stops:

 Left align the text by clicking the **Align Text Left** button on the **Paragraph** group on the **Home** tab of the Ribbon.

 Click on the Ruler at 60 mm and hold for a second or so.

Notice that an L shape appears at this point on the Ruler.

 Do the same at:

> 120 mm on the Ruler.

> 162.5 mm (the last mark on the Ruler before the page edge).

 Check that the tab stops work by using the **Tab** key to move across the page.

We are going to place the controls on the form, but before we can do this, you will have to make the Developer tab appear on the Ribbon.

 Click the Office button.

 Click **Word Options** (at the bottom of the dialogue box).

The Word Options dialogue box opens:

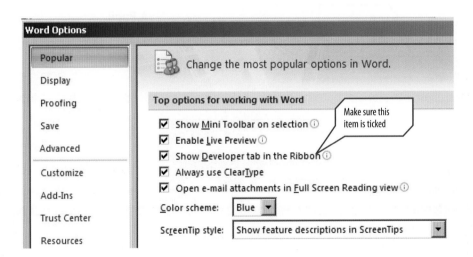

Figure 1.11

 Select **Popular**.

 Tick (click on) **Show Developer tab in the Ribbon**.

 Click **OK**.

29 Swap to the **Developer** tab:

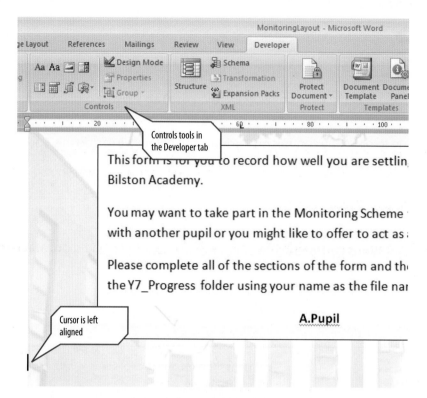

Figure 1.12

There are eight control boxes to add – let's make a start.

Control box 1 – Name

Look at Figure 1.3 on page 14; we need to put a control suitable to hold someone's name on the left. This is how you do it:

 30 Make sure that the insertion point cursor is on the left as shown in Figure 1.12.

31 Click the **Rich Text** control button in the **Control** group.

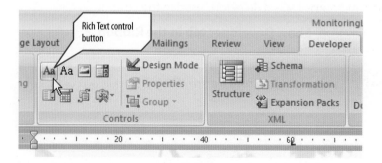

Figure 1.13

The control is inserted in the form:

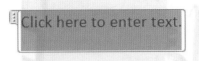

Figure 1.14

The control looks pretty boring like this, though, so we need to make some changes to the control's appearance. This is done through changing the control's Properties:

 Click the **Properties** button.

 Type 'Name' in the **Title** box and tick (click) the **Use a style to format contents** box:

Content Control Properties ? X

General

Title: Name

Tag:

☑ Use a style to format contents

Style: Default Paragraph Font ▼

¶ New Style...

Locking

☐ Content control cannot be deleted

☐ Contents cannot be edited

Rich Text Properties

☐ Remove content control when contents are edited

OK   Cancel

Figure 1.15

Let's see if we can improve the style of font used in the control:

Click the **New Style** button.

The **Create New Style from Formatting** dialogue box opens:

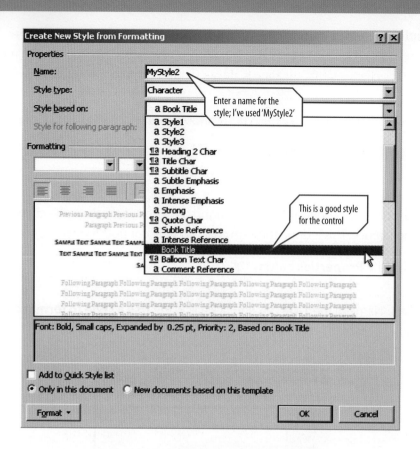

Figure 1.16

35 Make the settings as shown in Figure 1.16.

36 Click **OK**.

37 Let's see if it works. Try entering your name in the control. You'll need to click the control box first to do this. Have a look at Figure 1.17, which should make this clear.

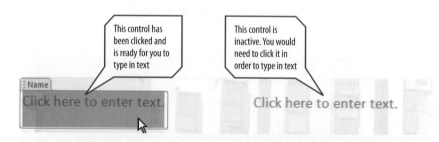

Figure 1.17

TIP

You don't need to delete the 'Click here to enter text' message before you start typing. Just type it in!

Control box 2 – Date

The next control we need to add to the form is the 'Date Picker'. This makes it easy to add the date and means that the date is always written in the same way.

38 Click just to the right of the name control and press the **Tab** key on the keyboard.

The cursor jumps to the new tab stop position at 60 mm:

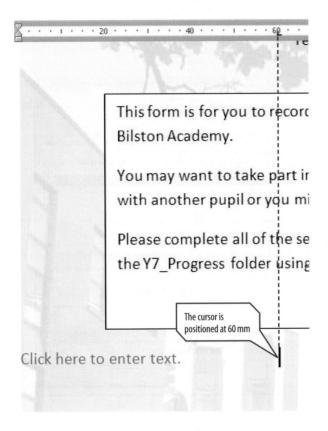

Figure 1.18

39 Click the **Date Picker** button on the **Developer** tab:

Figure 1.19

The Date Picker control arrives on the form.

40 Click the **Properties** button.

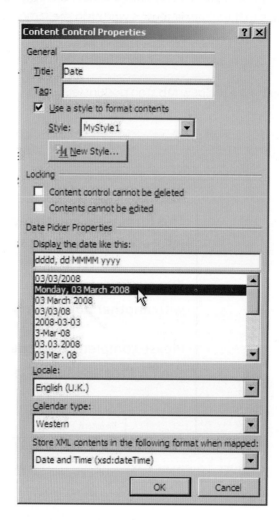

Figure 1.20

Copy the settings that you see in Figure 1.20.

41 Test the Date Picker control by changing to another date such as your birthday – unless that's today, in which case happy birthday!

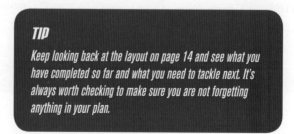

TIP

Keep looking back at the layout on page 14 and see what you have completed so far and what you need to tackle next. It's always worth checking to make sure you are not forgetting anything in your plan.

On to the next control.

Control box 3 – Best subject

The next control allows pupils to select their best subject from a list, but first you need to move down by *two* lines so that there is some space between the controls.

 Tab across to the end of the line and press the **Enter** key *twice*.

 Click the **Drop-Down List** button in the **Controls** group.

The control appears on the form but before it can be used you need to write in the subjects that the pupils can choose as their 'Best Subject':

Figure 1.21

 Type 'Best Subject' in the **Title** box.

 Tick (click) **Use a style to format contents** and click the drop-down menu to select the style you used in the previous controls.

46 Click the **Add...** button.

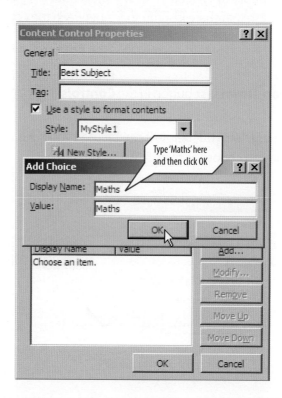

Figure 1.22

The **Add Choice** dialogue box loads.

47 Type 'Maths' into the **Display Name** box. Notice that the same subject appears in the Value box.

48 Click **OK**.

49 Maths appears as a subject in the **Drop-Down List Properties** box:

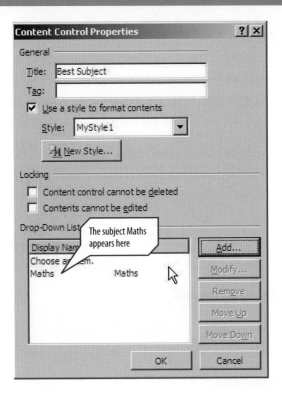

Figure 1.23

50 Now do the same to add the other subjects that you have on the Year 7 timetable.

51 Once you have added all of the subjects, click **OK**.

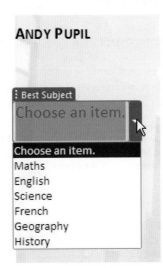

Figure 1.24

52 Now check that the drop-down list control works correctly and that you can select a subject.

On to the next control.

Control box 4 – Subject needing help

 53 The next control will be the same as the one we used for Best Subject except for its name so instead of re-doing everything you can copy the Best Subject control using the **Ctrl + C** method. Once you have copied it, tab to the new position and paste in the copy using the **Ctrl + V** method.

 54 Click the **Properties** button and change the **Title** to 'Subject needing help', then click **OK**. What you mean by this title is the subject the pupil is needing help with, but we need to keep the titles fairly short so the boxes don't take up too much space.

That was quick! We're getting good at this and we've nearly completed all of the controls we need – only a few more to go. This one is 'Help finding way around school'.

Control box 5 – Help finding way around

 55 Tab to the position of the next control (check your planning layout if you need to) and insert another Drop-Down List control.

 56 Click the **Properties** button.

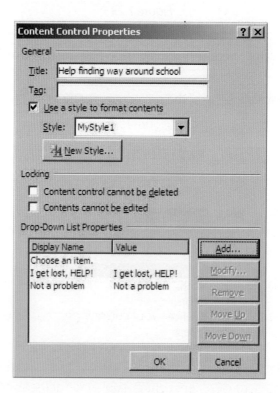

Figure 1.25

 57 Fill in the **Content Control Properties** as in Figure 1.25, then click **OK**.

On to the next box.

Control box 6 – Any problems

 58 Tab across to the end of the line and press the **Enter** key *twice*.

 59 Now tab across to the 60 mm tab.

 60 Insert another **Rich Text** control. `Aa`

 61 Set the properties as in Figure 1.26.

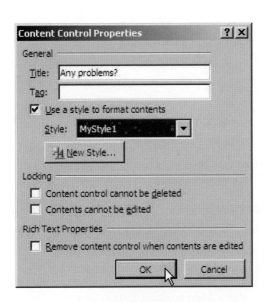

Figure 1.26

 62 When you have set the properties, click **OK**.

 63 Type in some text to check that the control works. If it does, we can move on. If not, retrace your steps and make sure that your controls match those in the book.

Before we tackle the last control box let's add a space for the image on the form.

 64 Tab across to the end of the line your cursor is on, press **Enter** *five* times then tab across to the 60 mm tab stop.

This point is now under the 'Any problems' Rich Text control and the place for inserting the Picture Content control. Look again at the layout in Figure 1.3.

Control box 7 – Picture

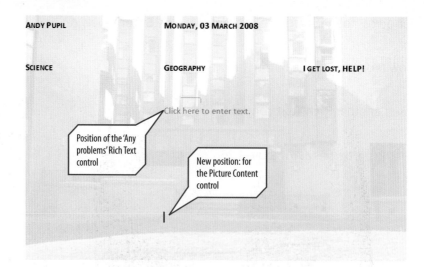

Figure 1.27

 Click the **Picture Content** control button to insert the control into the form.

 Click the **Properties** button.

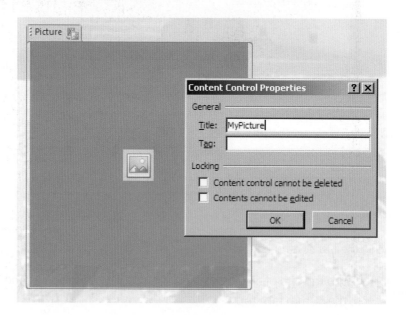

Figure 1.28

 You can use the title in Figure 1.28 or your own.

 Click **OK**.

Let's have a look at progress. You can see the form with 'test data' showing on it.

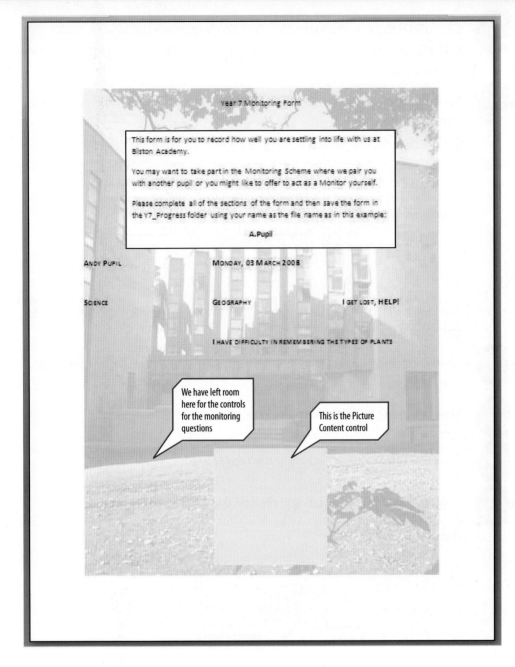

Figure 1.29

Now to the last controls to be added. These are the ones associated with peer monitoring.

Control box 8 – Peer monitoring

There are two questions for this section, each with a YES/NO answer. These are:

❯ Do you want to take part in the Monitoring Scheme?

❯ Do you want to offer to be a Monitor?

We can use a **Check Box** control for recording pupils' answers to these questions. A tick will mean 'Yes' and a blank box will mean a 'No' answer.

Click under the 'Any Problems' Rich Text box and type 'PEER MONITORING SERVICE'. The writing will be in capitals because of the style you set earlier on; we can change this later.

 Click on the right indent marker on the Ruler (see Figure 1.30) and drag it to 50 mm on the Ruler.

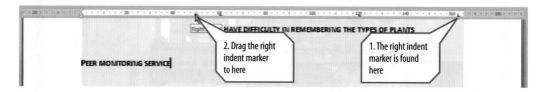

2. Drag the right indent marker to here

1. The right indent marker is found here

PEER MONITORING SERVICE

Figure 1.30

The idea here is to limit the length of lines of text so they do not spread out to the right of the page.

 Press Enter and type in 'DO YOU WANT TO TAKE PART IN THE MONITORING SCHEME?'

 Make another tab stop at 45 mm on the Ruler.

 Press the **Tab** key to tab across to the new tab stop.

 Swap to the **Developer** tab and click on the **Legacy Tools** button.

The Legacy Toolbox opens:

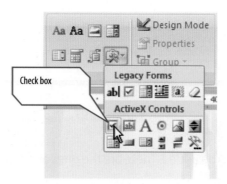

Check box

Figure 1.31

 Click the **Check Box Form Field** icon.

A check box is inserted into the form, but the screen looks a complete disaster! Don't worry, it is in 'Design Mode' and we can return the appearance to the original very easily. *Don't* try to change things around!

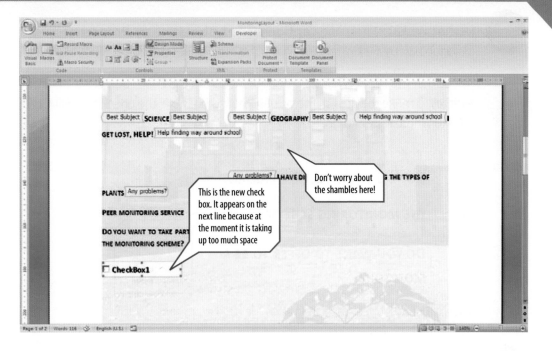

Figure 1.32

 Click the **Properties** button in the **Control** group.

The rather complex looking Properties dialogue box arrives, but we only have one thing to do in the box, so don't worry!

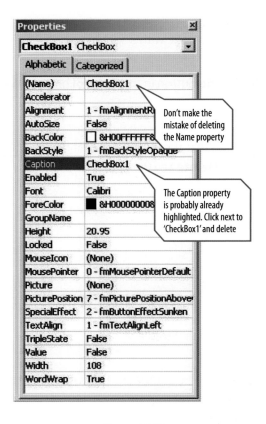

Figure 1.33

Delete CheckBox1 from the **Caption** property then close the **Properties** dialogue box by clicking the small x at the top right of the box.

Notice that the caption has now disappeared from the check box. Now drag the handles to make the area of the box as small as possible; the check box will jump back to where it should go:

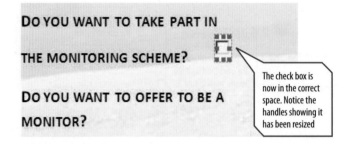

Figure 1.34

 Press **Enter** and type in:

'DO YOU WANT TO OFFER TO BE A MONITOR?'

 Tab across to the tab stop at 45 mm and insert another check box in the same way as the previous one. Don't forget to delete the caption (it will be called 'CheckBox2' this time).

Now we'll tackle the chaos on the page with a spot of tidying!

 Click the **Design Mode** button in the **Control** group.

Better?

 You will probably find that the Picture Content control has disappeared onto the next page. Press the **Delete** key (*not* the backspace) until the control reappears on the form.

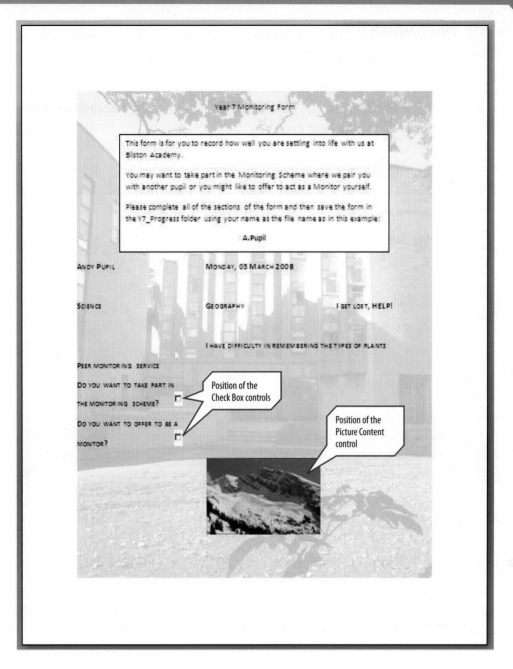

Figure 1.35

Save your work!

 Click on the Office button and then click **Save As**.

 In the Save As dialogue box, be sure that you select **Word Macro-Enabled Document** in the **Save as type** box; see Figure 1.36.

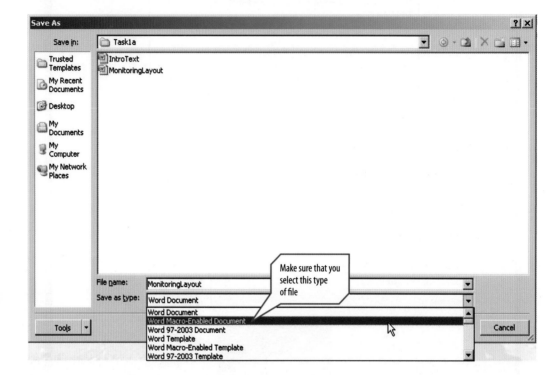

Figure 1.36

Well, that has been quite a job, but you have just about completed the layout. There is some tidying up to do, some of the text needs formatting but at this stage we should send a copy of the layout to Mrs Reynolds for her to check that what we have done meets her requirements. We will leave the other jobs for Task 2.

Test it!

FUNCTIONAL SKILLS

Reviewing work – at this stage we would look back at our plans and make sure we had included everything we needed to. Then we would check with our client (Mrs Reynolds) to make sure she was happy with the work so far in case she wanted any changes before we went ahead with the next stage

There are a few things that you could do before starting Task 2.

The most important is to check that the controls really do work. Here are some ideas:

❯ Reload the file and type in a name.

❯ Make different selections of date, subject, etc.

❯ Write some text in the 'Any problems' control.

❯ Save the file with a different name (such as MonitoringLayout_test).

❯ Open the file again and check that the contents are still in place.

Now write a brief report for Mrs Reynolds on the result of your test.

CHECKPOINT

Check that you know how to:

➤ Create new folders and files.

➤ Navigate to find a file.

➤ Add a watermark to a page.

➤ Use keyboard shortcuts to copy and paste.

➤ Add and adjust tab stops and indent markers.

➤ Insert a Rich Text control.

➤ Insert a Date Picker control.

➤ Insert a Drop-Down List control.

➤ Insert a Picture Content control.

➤ Insert a Check Box Form Field control.

➤ Set properties for each type of control.

➤ Save a file with a new file type.

ASSESSMENT POINT

Now let's assess the work. Look back at the table at the beginning of this section (**Target point**) and decide on which of the statements you can answer 'Yes' to.

Did you do as well as you expected? Could you improve your work? Use Word to write a comment to show what you could do to improve your work and remember this when starting your next ICT project.

GET AHEAD

Check out 'hyperlinks' using Microsoft Word 2007 help files. Find what they are used for – you are going to use them in Task 2!

Task 2

TASK BRIEF

The Head of Year 7 has sent you the following email...

BACKGROUND

You are now going to complete the form that you started in Task1. The term 'Formatting' is used to mean changing the appearance of a document. Before starting this, always ask yourself who is going to use the document and whether it is to be used in a formal setting such as a place of work, school, doctor's surgery, etc. Remember, you are not producing this work to please yourself; the form that you produce has a serious job to fulfil and the wrong formatting could make it less effective.

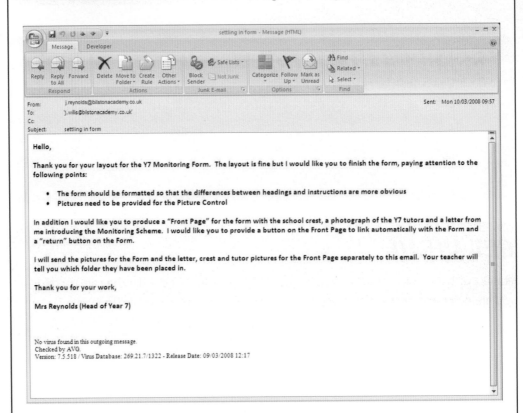

From: j.reynolds@bilstonacademy.co.uk **Sent:** Mon 10/03/2008 09:57
To: 'j.willis@bilstonacademy.co.uk'
Cc:
Subject: settling in form

Hello,

Thank you for your layout for the Y7 Monitoring Form. The layout is fine but I would like you to finish the form, paying attention to the following points:

- The form should be formatted so that the differences between headings and instructions are more obvious
- Pictures need to be provided for the Picture Control

In addition I would like you to produce a "Front Page" for the form with the school crest, a photograph of the Y7 tutors and a letter from me introducing the Monitoring Scheme. I would like you to provide a button on the Front Page to link automatically with the Form and a "return" button on the Form.

I will send the pictures for the Form and the letter, crest and tutor pictures for the Front Page separately to this email. Your teacher will tell you which folder they have been placed in.

Thank you for your work,

Mrs Reynolds (Head of Year 7)

No virus found in this outgoing message.
Checked by AVG.
Version: 7.5.518 / Virus Database: 269.21.7/1322 - Release Date: 09/03/2008 12:17

Figure 2.1

SOFTWARE SKILLS

You will learn how to:

> Format text and images
> Change a style
> Insert additional pages in a document
> Add hyperlinks to a document

FUNCTIONAL SKILLS

As you work through this task the Functional Skills tabs will explain to you why the task tackles this brief in the way shown here and explain why you would choose to:

> Use particular styles and fonts
> Edit images

CAPABILITY

You are not expected to show capability in this Task because you are following a set of instructions.

VOCABULARY

You should learn these new words and understand what they mean:

> Mode
> Formatting
> Aspect ratio
> Hyperlink
> Bookmark
> Hotspot

RESOURCES

There are 5 files for this task:

MonitoringLayout.docm

MonitoringLetter.docx

MonitoringPictures folder

MonitoringTutors.jpg

MonitoringCrest.jpg

You can download these files from www.payne-gallway.co.uk

 TARGET POINT

Turn the page to see your Target Points for this task.

TARGET POINT

Have a look at the following statements before you start your task so that you know what you are aiming for.

Although you will not make your own decisions on the formatting of the form in Task 2, you can use what you learn here to help with other work that will be awarded a particular level.

SOFTWARE SKILLS

Assembling related files in a folder

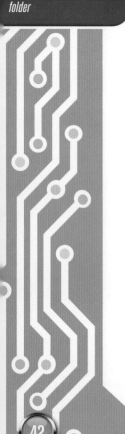

Level 3	Level 4	Level 5	Level 6
You have found and saved the files needed for this task	You have copied your files in folders with suitable names	You can say why it is important to save your files in particular folders	
You have followed the instructions to insert a picture	You have resized the picture to a suitable size for your document		
You have followed the instructions to insert a new page	You have changed the page using formatting tools to suit your plan	You have found and inserted suitable assets (images, text) onto your page	
You have followed the instructions to insert a bookmark or hotspot	You have inserted a bookmark and hotspot to make a hyperlink	You have tested the hyperlink and solved any problems	You have make decisions about which other hyperlinks would be suitable for your document

Before we start

Task 2 concentrates on the following activities:

❯ Formatting the form we made in Task 1 to make it more useful to the user.

❯ Adding a new page to the document.

❯ Linking pages using hyperlinks.

Organising your work

Before you start any task you should organise the area of the computer where you are going to save the work.

 Load Word 2007.

 Copy the following files and folders to your Monitoring folder:

❯ MonitoringLetter

❯ MonitoringPictures folder (it's best to copy and paste the whole folder into your Monitoring folder rather than copying the individual files because this will keep all of the images together)

❯ MonitoringTutors (An image of the Year 7 tutors)

❯ MonitoringCrest (An image of the School Crest)

 Open MonitoringLayout (the Layout from Task 1).

You may find that your form loads in 'Design Mode' and will not let you turn off Design Mode. If this is the case follow the instructions below.

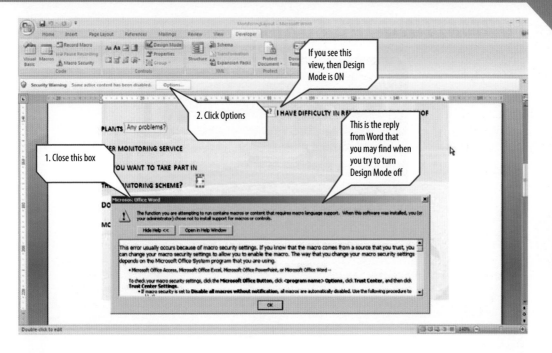

Figure 2.2

 Close the dialogue box and click on the **Options** button.

 In the **Microsoft Office Security Options** dialogue box, click **Enable this content**:

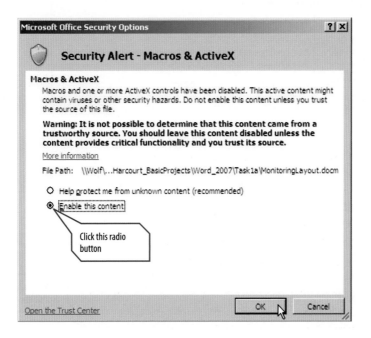

Figure 2.3

 Click **OK**.

After some seconds of dithering, the familiar view returns. Phew! At last, now you can get started.

FORMATTING THE FORM

SOFTWARE SKILLS
Formatting text

 Highlight the title and change the font to **Bold**, size **16**.

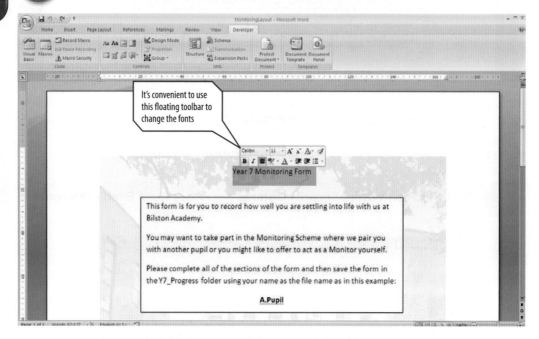

Figure 2.4

 Highlight 'PEER MONITORING SERVICE' and click the small arrow in the bottom right corner of the **Font** group on the **Home** tab:

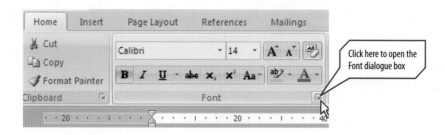

Figure 2.5

The **Font** dialogue box opens. Change the settings so yours appears as it does in Figure 2.6.

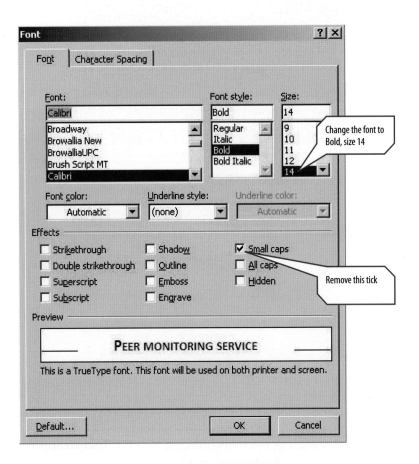

Figure 2.6

FUNCTIONAL SKILLS

Choosing an appropriate font for your audience and purpose is very important – as our form is a formal document used by the school and our audience will have a range of reading abilities we want to make sure we keep the font professional looking, and clear and large enough to make it easy to read. The font size for the heading is larger so that it stands out and makes the form easy to identify

TIP
You may find that the Picture control has disappeared onto the next page. If so, delete a line above 'Peer monitoring service'.

 Now for each of the questions about monitoring alter the fonts used to **lower case** (remove the tick in the Small caps box), **Bold**, size **11** in the same way as you did for the 'Peer monitoring' heading.

The 'Peer monitoring' group of questions could be improved by appearing to be surrounded by a box so that the questions look like they belong together.

 Swap to the Insert tab and click the **Shapes** icon.

 Choose the **Rectangle** shape:

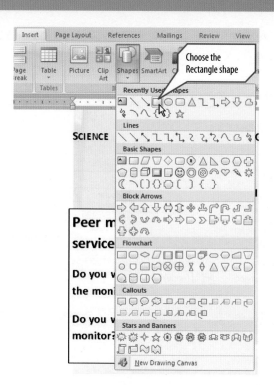

Figure 2.7

12 Use the cross-wire cursor to draw a rectangle over the 'Peer monitoring' area.

Help! It's all gone wrong! Don't panic, this is easy to sort out.

13 The rectangle should be still highlighted, so click the **Text Wrapping** icon in the **Arrange** group of the **Format** tab and follow the instructions on Figure 2.8.

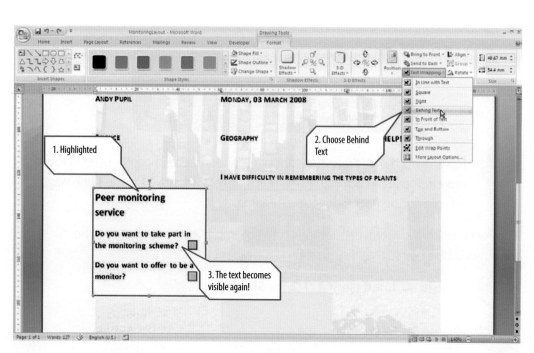

Figure 2.8

The 'Peer monitoring' section now looks better because it is clear and can be easily understood by any user.

Now let's look at the Picture control box.

Testing the Picture Content control
Let's see if we can change the image.

 Click in the **Picture Content** control to make it active:

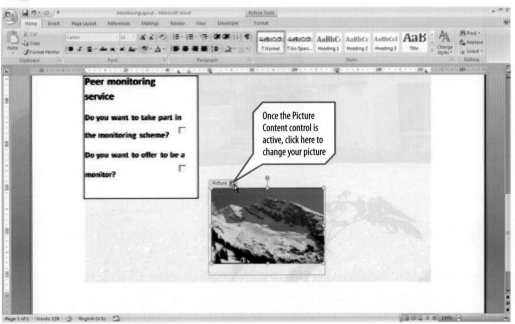

Figure 2.9

 Use the **Insert Picture** dialogue box to navigate to your MonitoringPictures folder:

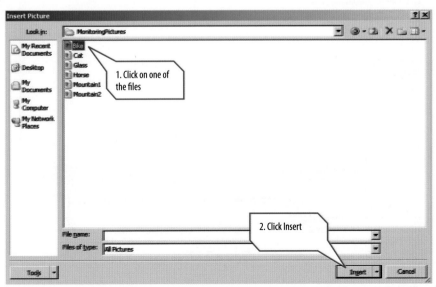

Figure 2.10

The picture appears inside the Picture Content control:

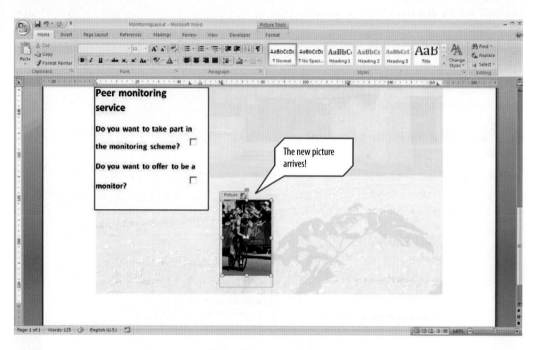

Figure 2.11

 Test the system by changing the picture and the other details for the pupil.

 Save your work as MonitoringLayout1. We will be making some changes to the document and, if anything goes wrong, we will need this file to be able to go back to. Remember, you need to save the file as the following type.

Word Macro-Enabled Document

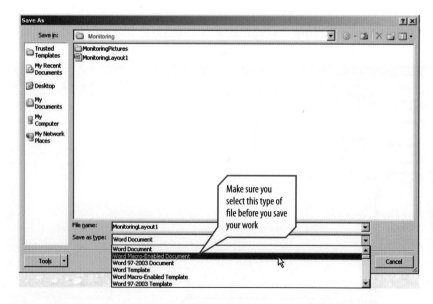

Figure 2.12

 Click **Save**.

A cover story

We are going to create a page that will sit before our form that we have just created. This is called a cover page and includes the important details about the project, like your name, the title of the project and the project brief.

We can save some work by using a preformed cover page from Word.

 Swap to the **Insert** tab and click the **Cover Page** icon in the **Pages** group.

There are several cover sheet templates to choose from, but the simple one called 'Stacks' is probably the most useful and appropriate for this formal document.

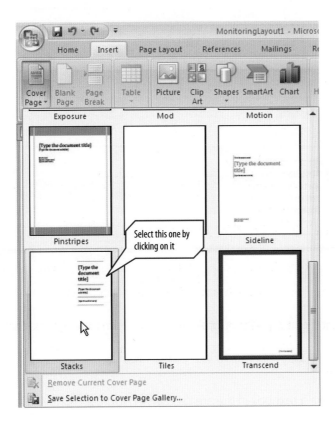

Figure 2.13

 Click on your choice.

 The new front page loads and appears on the screen.

SOFTWARE SKILLS

Adding a new page to a document

Adding content to a page in the form of pre-formed text and pictures.

FUNCTIONAL SKILLS

Many documents that you produce for a particular purpose will have a layout that is thought of as a standard style which you should follow. To make things easier and quicker you can find templates in Word that show you how to set your document out. Here we are using a template for a cover sheet

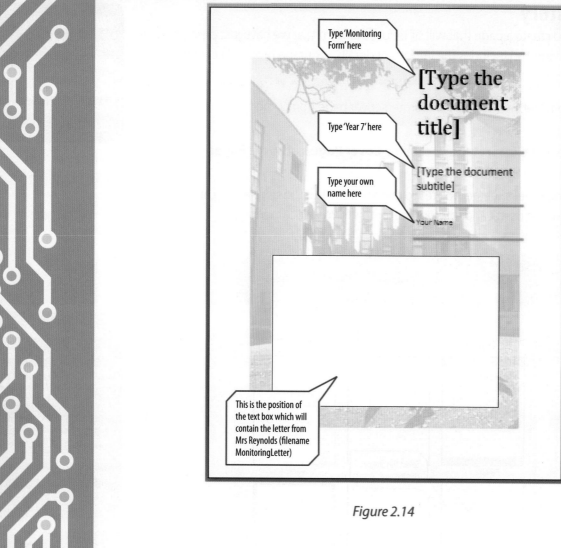

Figure 2.14

You will notice that the new page is a form with controls similar to the one that you have made.

22 Type in the changes shown in Figure 2.14.

23 Now make a text box in the area shown in Figure 2.14. Have a look back at Task 1 if you are not sure how to do this.

24 Navigate to the file MonitoringLetter and transfer the letter to the text box as you did with the Instructions in Task 1.

> **TIP**
> *If you find that the contents of the Insert tab are all 'greyed out' and unavailable, swap to the Developer tab and click Design Mode on and off once.*

25 Now transfer the crest (filename MonitoringCrest) and the picture of the Year 7 tutors (filename MonitoringTutors).

The picture will be far too big when it appears on the screen, so…

 26   Swap to the **Format** tab (you will probably have this in focus at the moment).

 27   Open the **Size** dialogue box by clicking the small diagonally downward-pointing arrow on the bottom right-hand side of the **Size** group:

Figure 2.15

 28   In the **Size and rotate** pane in the **Size** dialogue box set the height to 40 mm; see Figure 2.16.

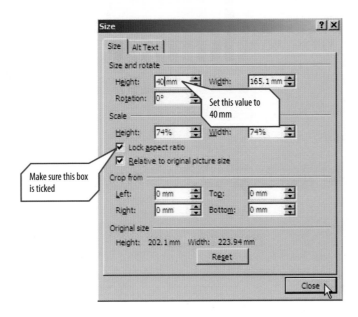

Figure 2.16

 29   Don't bother with the **Width** setting. Word will sort this out for you providing you tick (click) **Lock aspect ratio**.

 30   Click **Close**.

 31   Set the **Text Wrapping** (see Figure 2.8 for details) to **Square**. Don't worry about the text box if it has disappeared!

 32   Move the school crest to the top left of the watermark on the page.

33 Import the picture of the Year 7 tutors (MonitoringTutors) in the same way and set the **Height** to **40 mm** and **Text Wrapping** to **Square**.

34 Move the picture of the tutors so that it is positioned below the crest (see Figure 2.19).

35 Swap to the **Format** tab and, using the samples in the **Picture Styles** group, select **Soft Edge Rectangle** to blend the crest and tutor pictures with the watermark background.

36 Reposition the text box and make sure that there is about 12 mm of the watermark showing at the bottom of the text box.

37 Swap to the **Format** tab and select **Shape Fill** in the **Text Box Styles** group:

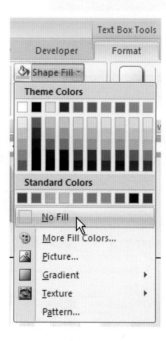

Figure 2.17

38 Select **No Fill**.

The letter becomes 'transparent' and the background watermark is visible through it.

39 Now select **Shape Outline** and click on **No Outline** in the drop-down list:

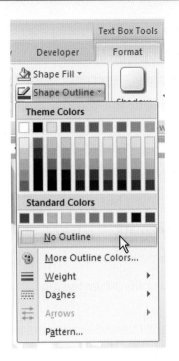

Figure 2.18

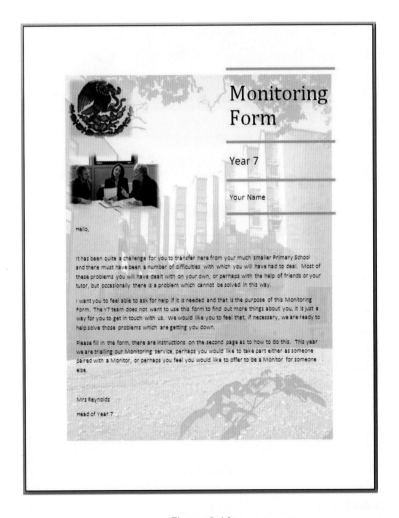

Figure 2.19

HYPERLINKS

We are going to make it possible for form users to move automatically from the cover page to the form.

We are going to use **hyperlinks** to do this. You have probably used hyperlinks to move from one web page to the next when you have been browsing the Internet, but we can also use the same technique to help users to move through pages in a Word document.

Each hyperlink consists of 2 parts:

❯❯ The starting point, which is also a **hotspot**.

❯❯ The end point, called a **bookmark**.

We will concentrate on the bookmark first.

40 Scroll down the screen until you see the top part of the form.

41 Click just to the left of the title and swap to the **Insert** tab on the Ribbon.

SOFTWARE SKILLS
Inserting a bookmark

42 Click the **Bookmark** button in the **Links** group:

Figure 2.20

43 Type the bookmark name 'Monitoring' in the **Bookmark** dialogue box:

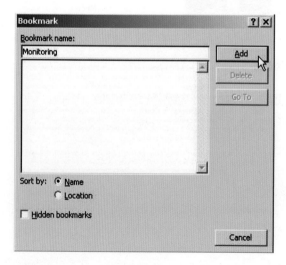

Figure 2.21

44 Click **Add**.

Now scroll back to the space at the bottom of the letter on the cover page.

 Swap to the **Insert** tab and draw a shape such as a **Block Arrow** at the bottom of the page underneath the letter.

 Choose one of the **Shape Styles** for the arrow:

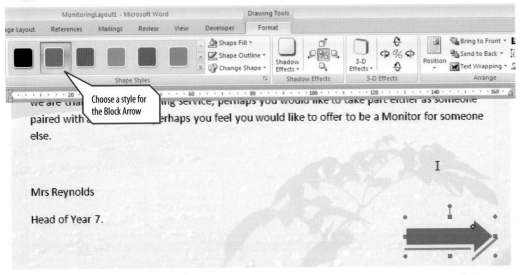

Figure 2.22

SOFTWARE SKILLS
Inserting shapes

 Swap to the **Insert** tab on the Ribbon.

 Make sure that the Block Arrow is still highlighted and click the **Hyperlink** button in the **Links** group.

 In the **Edit Hyperlink** dialogue box, click the option **Place in This Document** (on the left-hand pane).

 Open the **Bookmarks** navigation and click **Monitoring**:

SOFTWARE SKILLS
Inserting a hotspot

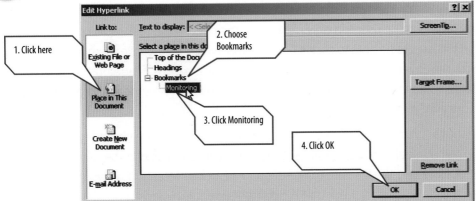

Figure 2.23

52 Click **OK**.

53 Now test the hyperlink by clicking off the **Block Arrow** to remove its highlight and then hover your mouse pointer over the shape:

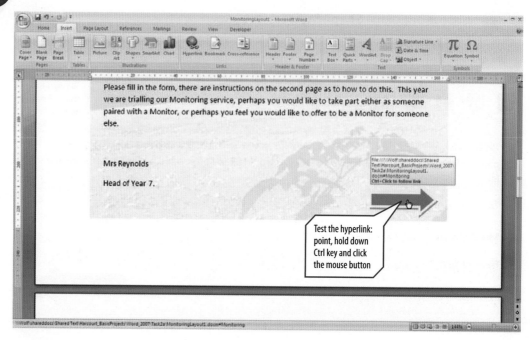

Figure 2.24

54 Hold down the **Ctrl** key and click the **Block Arrow**.

Bingo! You are transported to the form on the next page!

Test it!

There are a few things that you could do before starting Task 3.

The most important is to check that the Hyperlink works correctly. If it doesn't, it is probably best to delete the Hotspot and the Bookmark and just start again.

There are no instructions for the user on the Hotspot: can you improve on this?

At the moment, the user can only move from the cover page to the form. It might be useful for users to be able to click a 'Back' button, which would take them from the form back to the cover page. Another idea for a hyperlink is a 'Top of Page' button. Applying your understanding and skills shows that you really have learnt new ideas and you are able to demonstrate your capability.

Save the file once you are sure it works correctly, then reload the file and type in a name, make some selections of date, subject, etc., and write some text in the 'Any problems' control. Now save the file with a different name (such as MonitoringLayout_testTask2). Open the file again and check that the contents are still in place.

Now write a brief report for Mrs Reynolds on the result of your improvements and tests.

CHECKPOINT

Check that you know how to:

➤ Assemble related files in a folder.

➤ Alter security properties affecting a document.

➤ Format text.

➤ Add a new page to a document.

➤ Add content to a page in the form of pre-formed text and pictures.

➤ Transfer files between documents such as the letter from Mrs Reynolds.

➤ Format pictures.

➤ Insert a bookmark.

➤ Insert shapes (e.g. Text Box, Block Arrow).

➤ Insert a hotspot.

➤ Test and use a hyperlink.

ASSESSMENT POINT

Now let's assess the work. Look back at the table at the beginning of this section (**Target point**) and decide on which of the statements you can answer 'Yes' to.

Did you do as well as you expected? Could you improve your work? Use Word to write a comment to show what you could do to improve your work and remember this when starting your next ICT project.

GET AHEAD

➤ Use the **Shapes** (**Insert** tab) to make a block diagram to show how the monitoring system will work.

➤ How will Mrs Reynolds know if the system is working correctly?

➤ How can Mrs Reynolds show the Headmaster, Mr Fryer, the success or failure of the monitoring system?

TASK BRIEF

The Head of Year 7
has sent you this email…

BACKGROUND

You are now going to produce a report. As before, to save on the amount of work that needs to be done we shall use a template. It is quite likely that Mrs Reynolds will have to write another report about the Peer Monitoring Service, so we will save time for her in the future by using form controls to hold the images and text in the correct place in the report. When she needs to write a new report, all she will need to do is delete the old images and text and insert the new ones. Simple!

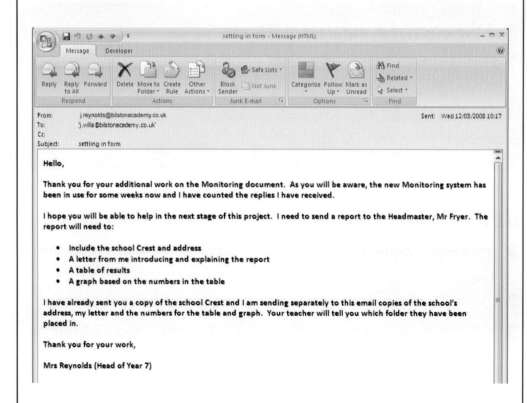

From: j.reynolds@bilstonacademy.co.uk   **Sent:** Wed 12/03/2008 10:17
To: 'j.willis@bilstonacademy.co.uk'
Cc:
Subject: settling in form

Hello,

Thank you for your additional work on the Monitoring document. As you will be aware, the new Monitoring system has been in use for some weeks now and I have counted the replies I have received.

I hope you will be able to help in the next stage of this project. I need to send a report to the Headmaster, Mr Fryer. The report will need to:

- Include the school Crest and address
- A letter from me introducing and explaining the report
- A table of results
- A graph based on the numbers in the table

I have already sent you a copy of the school Crest and I am sending separately to this email copies of the school's address, my letter and the numbers for the table and graph. Your teacher will tell you which folder they have been placed in.

Thank you for your work,

Mrs Reynolds (Head of Year 7)

Figure 3.1

SOFTWARE SKILLS

You will learn how to:

> Modify a template containing controls
> Use WordArt
> Insert and use a table
> Insert a graph

FUNCTIONAL SKILLS

As you work through this task the Functional Skills tabs will explain to you why the task tackles this brief in the way shown here and explain why you would choose to:

> Use a template
> Combine information from different sources
> Display information as a graph
> Use tables

CAPABILITY

You are not expected to show capability in this Task because you are following a set of instructions.

VOCABULARY

You should learn these new words and understand what they mean:

> Merge
> Formula
> Category
> Percentage

RESOURCES

There are 4 files for this task:

ReportLetter.docx

ReportAddress.docx

ReportNumbers.docx

MonitoringCrest.jpg

You can download these files from www.payne-gallway.co.uk

 TARGET POINT

Turn the page to see your Target Points for this task.

TARGET POINT

Have a look at the following statements before you start your task so that you know what you are aiming for.

Although you will not make your own decisions in this task, you can use what you learn here to help with other work that will be awarded a particular level.

Level 3	Level 4	Level 5	Level 6
You have found and saved the files needed for this task	You have copied your files in folders with suitable names	You can say why it is important to save your files in particular folders	You can say why you should save different versions of a document each time to make major changes
You have followed the instructions to use WordArt	You have used the editing features to change a WordArt title suitable for your document	You have used the editing features to change a WordArt title and make it suitable for your document	
You have followed the instructions to insert a table	You have changed the table using formatting tools to suit your plan	You have designed your table to be suitable for your document	
You have followed the instructions to insert a chart (graph)	You have changed the chart to display data from the table	You have added detail to the chart to help users understand its purpose	You have created a new chart suitable for your data

Before we start

Task 3 is focused on writing a report on the Peer Monitoring Service for the Headmaster of Bilston Academy and you will be:

> Designing a document based on a template.

> Incorporating other assets (the letter, address and school crest) in the new report.

> Using WordArt.

> Making a table to hold and calculate the results from the Peer Monitoring survey.

> Making a graph to display the results from the table.

Organising your work

Before you start any task you should organise the area of the computer where you are going to save the work.

You need to set up a folder for all of the files you need and move files to this new folder.

 Load Word 2007.

 Navigate to your Monitoring folder and make a new folder called 'Report'. This is the folder that will contain all of the files used in making the report and, eventually, the report itself.

 Navigate to your Monitoring folder and copy the MonitoringCrest file.

 Paste the file into your Report folder.

5 Navigate to where the other files you need are stored. The files you need to copy and paste into your Report folder are:

> ReportLetter

> ReportAddress

> ReportNumbers

6 Check that you have all of the assets (the files that you will need) in your Report folder.

You will notice that you save copies of the work as it progresses. Do you remember why this is good practice? Remember – because if you make a mistake or for some reason the file you are working on is lost, there will always be another copy made at an earlier stage. This way you won't lose all of your work even if things go wrong.

Right, time to get started!

CHOOSE A TEMPLATE

I have mentioned before how a well-chosen template can save you time and effort – this task is no exception.

7 Click the Office button and then click **New**.

The **New Document** dialogue box loads:

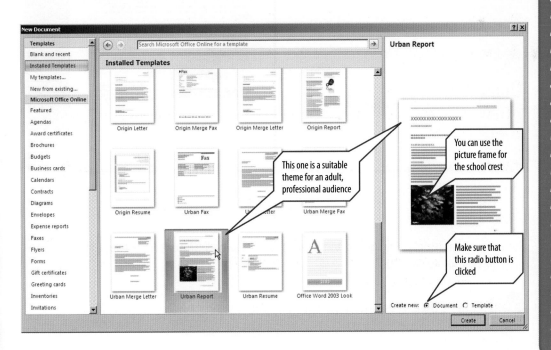

Figure 3.2

FUNCTIONAL SKILLS

Choosing templates – we are producing a report for the Headmaster that will show the results of the survey that we produced in Tasks 1 and 2, so we need to choose our template to match our audience and purpose. We have chosen one that allows us to include images (as we will insert the school crest and a graph) and several paragraphs of text in a single column (a double column would make it look more like a newsletter or magazine and we want our document to look more formal than that). It also allows space for the name of the author, which appears as a 'header' (so a reader will know who has written the document and could identify them if they have questions about the information). We can include a date so they know how recently the report was written

By using the right template for the right purpose it helps your readers to know how to respond – does it look like a formal report that might contain important information that they must read; does it look like a newsletter that contains less important information?

 8   In the left-hand pane of the box, select **Installed Templates** then select **Urban Report**.

 9   Click **Create**.

SOFTWARE SKILLS

Changing and reusing a pre-formed template

THE TEMPLATE LAYOUT

The template loads, but you can't see much of it. We will need to have a quick look at the whole document before starting.

 10   Swap to the **View** tab and click the **Full Screen Reading** button in the **Document Views** group.

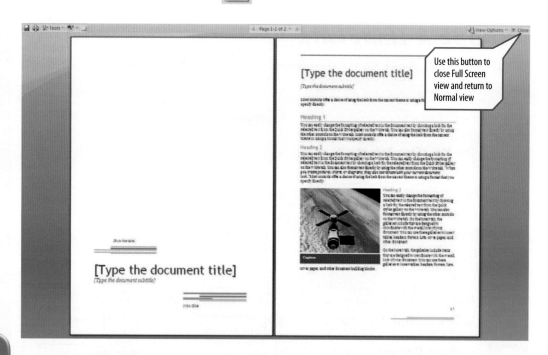

Figure 3.3

FUNCTIONAL SKILLS

As well as checking that your paper is the correct size for your printer, you should also check that it is 'portrait' as this is the most suitable format for a report

This document is probably going to be printed, so we had better check that the page size is correct for an A4 printer.

 11   Click **Close** to return to the Normal view.

12   Swap to the **Page Layout** tab and click the **Size** button:

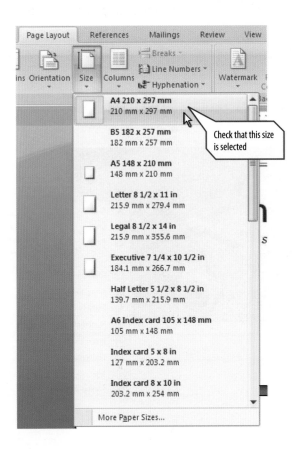

Figure 3.4

It seems a bit of a mystery why you can't move the picture to the front page until you realise that the template is a series of controls. You need to turn on Design Mode before you can move the picture.

 13   Swap to the **Developer** tab (if the Developer tab is not on the Ribbon, look back at Task 1, page 21, which shows you how to switch it on).

14   Click the **Design Mode** button. ✎ Design Mode

 15   Drag the picture (in my version it shows the International Space Station) to the top left of the first page.

Now we'll exchange the space station for the school crest picture:

 Right click on the picture.

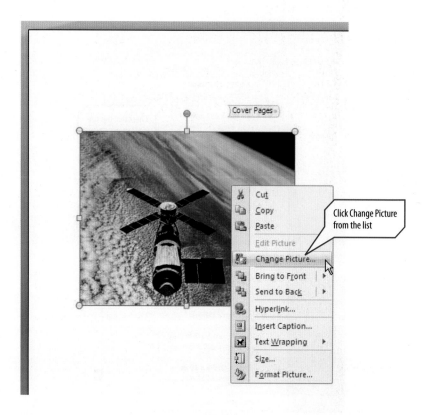

Figure 3.5

 Use the **Insert Picture** dialogue box to navigate to your Report folder:

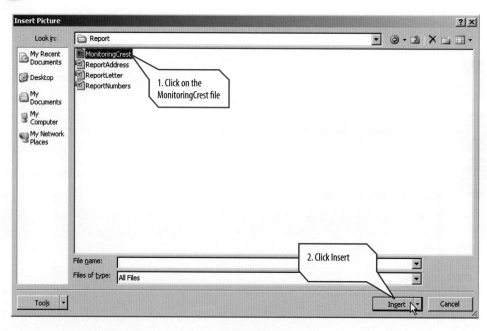

Figure 3.6

Click on the filename as shown in Figure 3.6 and then click **Insert**.

 Try to turn off Design View.

You can't! Instead you get this error report:

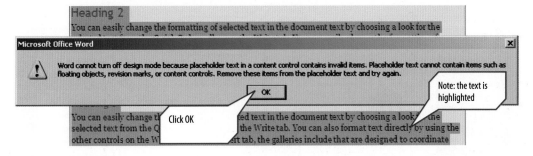

Figure 3.7

 Clear the error message by clicking on **OK**.

The text (which of course will not be needed because we will replace it with the report letter) will be highlighted and can now be deleted:

 Press the **Delete** button on the keyboard.

 Now you can turn off Design Mode.

Next on the menu is the heading which should feature the name of the school. You can't easily write directly into this template as it is largely covered with controls that prevent you from writing anywhere.

The way around this is to use a text box to contain the heading.

 Draw a text box (**Insert** > **Shapes** > **Text Box**) as in Figure 3.8.

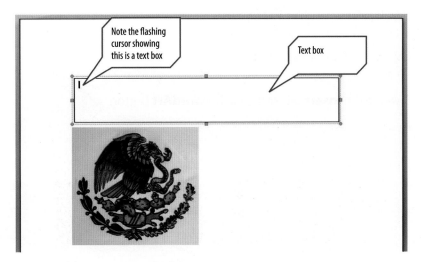

Figure 3.8

24 Draw another text box just to the right of the school crest to contain the address.

Let's see if we have completed the layout:

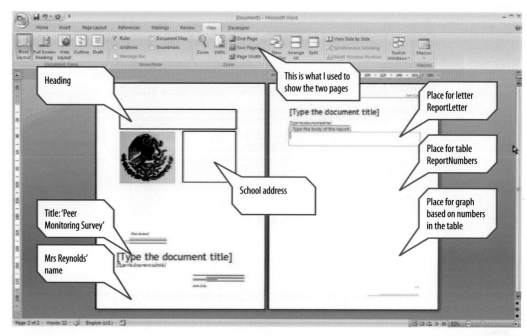

Heading

This is what I used to show the two pages

Place for letter ReportLetter

[Type the document title]

Place for table ReportNumbers

School address

Place for graph based on numbers in the table

Title: 'Peer Monitoring Survey'

Mrs Reynolds' name

[Type the document title]

Figure 3.9

It looks as if we have places for all of the items we need to include, so we can move on to formatting.

25 Save your work. Save the file as a Word document with the filename **Report_PeerMonitoring1**.

Formatting the heading
We are going to use WordArt for the heading.

26 Click in the **Heading** text box.

27 Swap to the **Insert** tab and click the **WordArt** button.

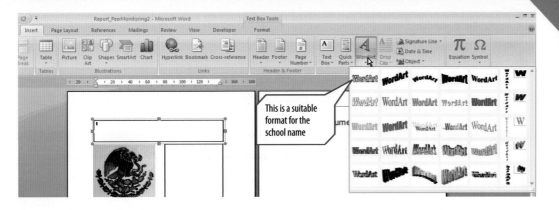

Figure 3.10

 Choose **WordArt Style 1** by clicking on the style.

 The **Edit WordArt** dialogue box loads:

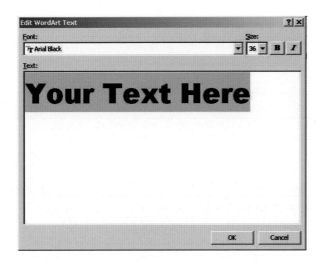

Figure 3.11

 Just type in 'Bilston Academy'; the text will replace 'Your Text Here'.

 Click **OK**.

Chances are that the title does not fill all of the text box so let's change this:

 Drag the text box out to cover the width of the page without going into the margins.

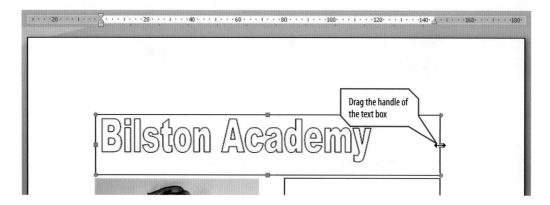

Drag the handle of the text box

Figure 3.12

 Click in the WordArt title to make it highlighted:

Drag this handle to the right hand side of the text box

Figure 3.13

 Drag the WordArt highlight handle to the right, so that the whole text box is filled with the WordArt highlight; see Figure 3.13.

The text expands to fill the whole width of the text box.

 Save your work. Save the file as a Word document with the filename **Report_PeerMonitoring2**.

Formatting the address

First you need to copy the address and paste it into the **Address** text box.

 Click the Office button and then choose **Open**:

Figure 3.14

 Use the **Open** dialogue box to navigate to and open the ReportAddress file:

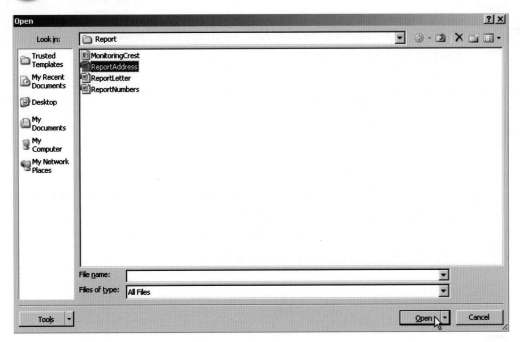

Figure 3.15

 When the ReportAddress file opens, highlight the text of the address:

Bilston Academy,
Bilston Road,
BILSTON,
HZ50 1QT.

Figure 3.16

 On your keyboard, hold down the **Ctrl** key and press **C** (copy).

 Close the ReportAddress file; you have finished using it now.

 Click in the Address text box on the front page of your report.

 On your keyboard, hold down the **Ctrl** key and press **V** (paste).

Well, the text is there, but it needs formatting.

 Highlight the address again and format the text to **Arial** font, size **22**, **Bold**.

 Save your work. Save the file as a Word document with the filename **Report_PeerMonitoring3**.

Formatting the date

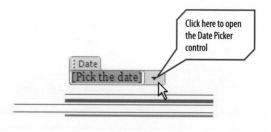 Click on the **Date Picker** control 'Pick the Date'.

Click here to open the Date Picker control

Date
[Pick the date]

Figure 3.17

 Click on the downward-pointing arrow to open the Date Picker control:

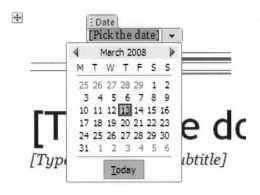

Figure 3.18

Check that the Date Picker control is still highlighted. It's easy to spot because it has 'Date' with a blue background above the actual date.

 Swap to the **Developer** tab and click the **Properties** button.

 Change the formatting in the **Properties** dialogue box as it appears in Figure 3.19.

Figure 3.19

 Click **OK**.

50 Test the control by selecting different dates such as your birthday and Christmas Day.

51 Finally, click on **Today**.

52 Save your work. Save the file as a Word document with the filename **Report_PeerMonitoring4**.

Formatting the document title, subtitle and author

53 Click on **Type the document title**.

It is obvious that this, too, is a control; so just:

54 Type in 'Peer Monitoring'.

55 Click on the **Subtitle** control.

56 Type in 'Survey Report'.

57 Click on the **Author** control and highlight the contents (which may be your own name, but remember that this report is from Mrs Reynolds, not you)!

58 Type in Mrs J. Reynolds. There is no need to delete your own name first.

59 Move down to the second page of the report.

After a bit of thinking, the computer updates the second sheet with the title, subtitle and author. More work saved!

60 Save your work. Save the file as a Word document with the filename **Report_PeerMonitoring5**.

Formatting the letter

61 Click in the control which is below the subtitle on the second page:

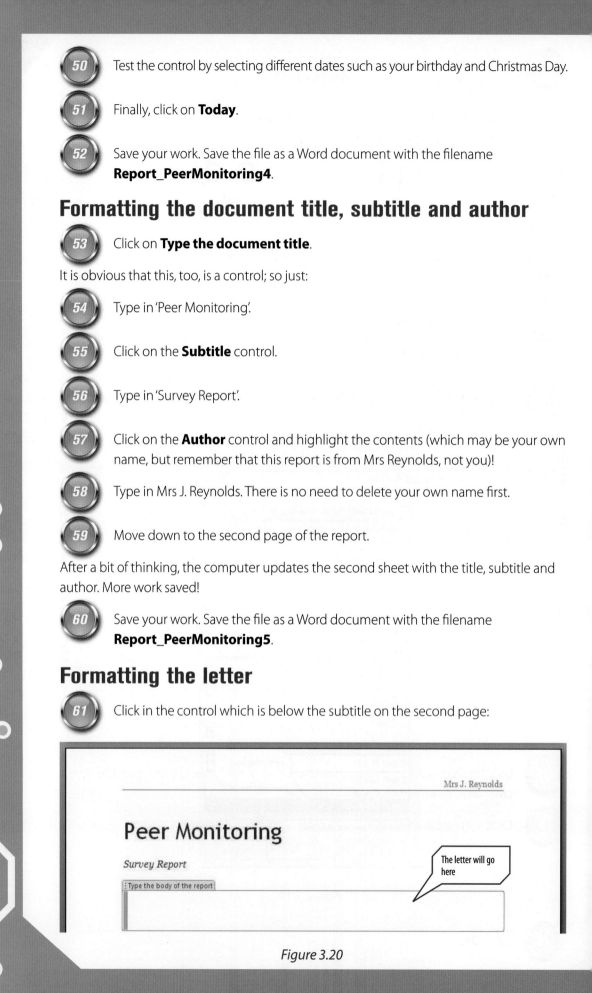

Figure 3.20

62 Paste in the letter (filename ReportLetter) in the same way as you did for the school address.

 63 Save your work. Save the file as a Word document with the filename **Report_PeerMonitoring6**.

Formatting the table

 64 Click underneath the letter, then press **Enter** to leave a blank line.

 65 Swap to the **Insert** tab and click the **Table** button.

SOFTWARE SKILLS
Adding and formatting a table

FUNCTIONAL SKILLS

Displaying numbers – we have included a table with our numbers in because it makes it much clearer and easier to align with the description of the numbers. It also means that you can do some simple calculations on the numbers in your table without using a spreadsheet

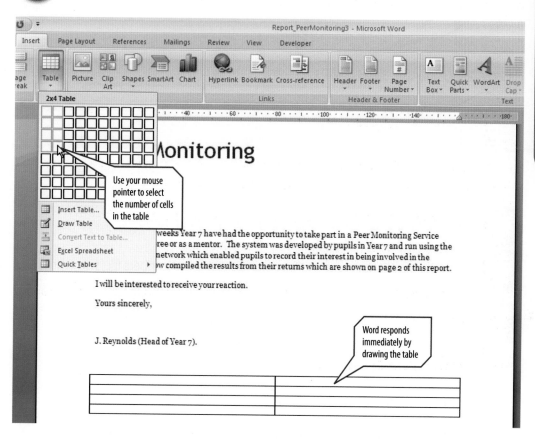

Figure 3.21

 66 Use the drop-down menu to choose the size of the table. You need a table with two columns and four rows.

 67 Click – the table appears in the report.

Navigate to the ReportNumbers file:

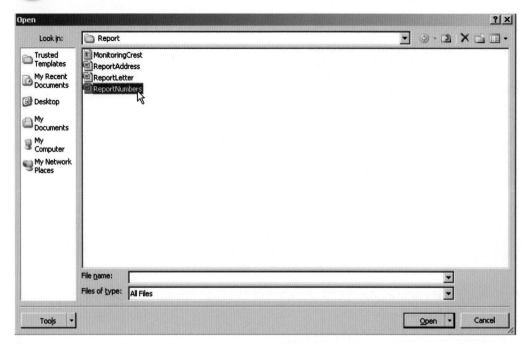

Figure 3.22

69 Open the ReportNumbers file; highlight the text and numbers.

70 Copy the highlighted text and then close the ReportNumbers file; you won't need it again.

71 Click in one of the cells of the table and paste in the copied text.

Disaster! It's all in one cell!

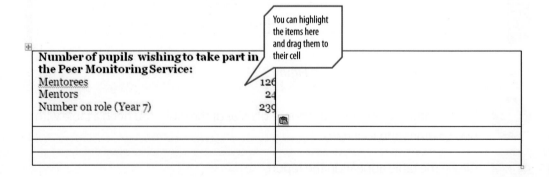

Figure 3.23

Highlight 'Number on roll (Year 7)' and drag to the left-hand column of the bottom row:

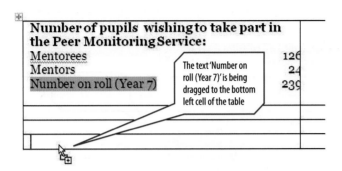

Figure 3.24

 Repeat this for the remaining items in the table; see Figure 3.25.

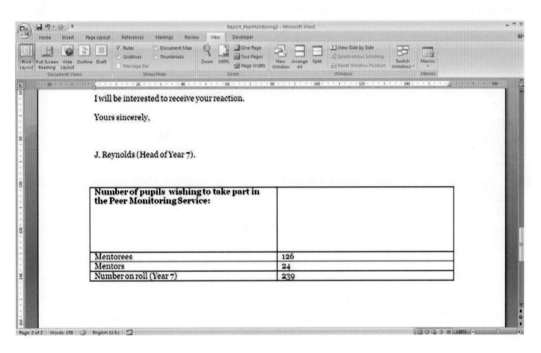

Figure 3.25

The title to the table would be better if it were spread across both columns:

 Highlight all of the top row and then click the right mouse button; see Figure 3.26 for further instructions.

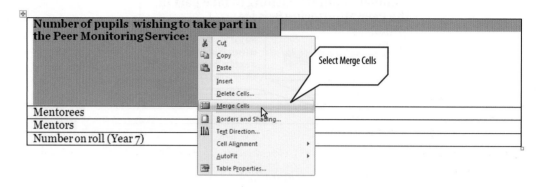

Figure 3.26

You will notice that the cell with the title is too deep, this is because there are extra lines below the text of the title. You can delete these now, which will tidy up the table.

It would be better if we also showed in the table the percentage of pupils wanting to take part as Mentorees and Mentors.

We need another column in our table to contain the new figures:

 Highlight the cells containing the numbers **126** and **24**.

 Swap to the **Table Tools**, **Layout** tab (careful – *not* the Page Layout tab).

 Click the **Split Cells** button in the **Merge** group:

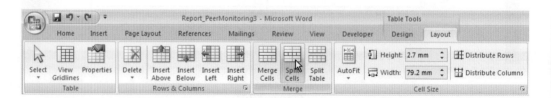

Figure 3.27

 Fill in the **Split Cells** dialogue box as shown in Figure 3.28.

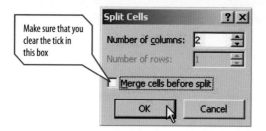

Make sure that you clear the tick in this box

Figure 3.28

79 Click **OK**.

You now need to work out the formula to calculate the percentage of pupils wanting to be mentored. It's quite simple really; the first thing to do is to work out the fraction of pupils wanting to be mentored:

$$\frac{\textbf{Number of mentorees}}{\textbf{Number on roll (Year 7)}}$$

If we multiply this fraction by 100, this will be the fraction out of 100 – in other words, the percentage of pupils wanting to be mentored:

$$\frac{\textbf{Number of mentorees}}{\textbf{Number on roll (Year 7)}} \times \textbf{100}$$

80 Click in the new cell to the right of 126.

81 Make sure you have the **Table Tools**, **Layout** tab on the top of the Ribbon and then click the **Formula** button. fx

82 Fill in the **Formula** dialogue box as shown in Figure 3.29.

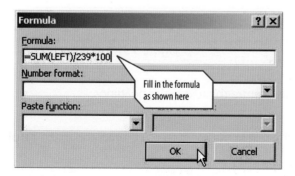

Fill in the formula as shown here

Figure 3.29

83 Click **OK**.

Repeat the formula for the cell to the right of 24.

Be careful that you write the formula for this cell exactly as shown in Figure 3.29.

It would be useful to have headings for the columns of the table.

 Highlight the row below the title of the table.

 Click the **Insert Above** button in the **Rows & Columns** group of the **Layout** tab. ▦

 Type in the headings and make them **bold** as in Figure 3.30.

Number of pupils wishing to take part in the Peer Monitoring Service:		
	Numbers of pupils	**Percentage of Year 7**
Mentorees	126	52.72
Mentors	24	10.04
Number on role (Year 7)	239	

> You may find that the text does not fit the column, as here

Figure 3.30

 Adjust the width of the columns by pointing to the line of the column, clicking and dragging as shown in Figure 3.31.

pupils	Percentage 7
	52.72
	10.04

Point to the line, click and drag

Figure 3.31

 Highlight and centre the text in the headings.

 Highlight the text in the 'Mentorees' column and make it **bold**.

 Highlight all of the text in the table and format it to **Arial** size **12**.

92 Click in the line we left above the table and type in the title for the table, as in Figure 3.32.

Peer Monitoring Survey

Number of pupils wishing to take part in the Peer Monitoring Service		
	Numbers of pupils	**Percentage of Year 7**
Mentorees	126	52.72
Mentors	24	10.04
Number on role (Year 7)	239	

Figure 3.32

 93 Swap to the **View** tab and click the **Full Screen Reading** button.

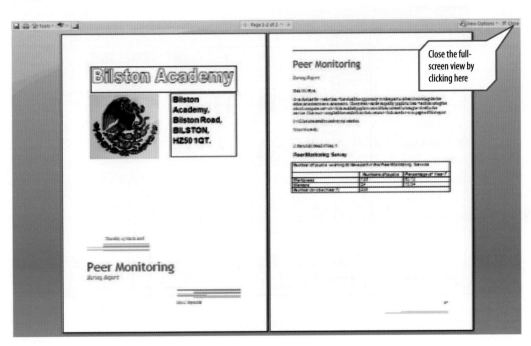

Figure 3.33

 94 Save your work. Save the file as a Word document with the filename **Report_PeerMonitoring7**.

FUNCTIONAL SKILLS

Inserting charts – we have displayed our numbers (figures) in a table so far but if we want to compare figures with one another, it is much easier to see the difference between them if they are displayed as a graph. Choosing the style of your graph or chart is important. We have chosen a bar chart because we want to show the difference between two single numbers

Formatting the graph (or chart)

This is the fun part of this project, so be prepared!

> **TIP**
>
> *You could draw a chart to show the percentages that we worked out – for that you should use a pie chart.*

 Click below the table.

 Swap to the **Insert** tab and click the **Chart** button.

97 In the **Insert Chart** dialogue box select the **Clustered Column** style:

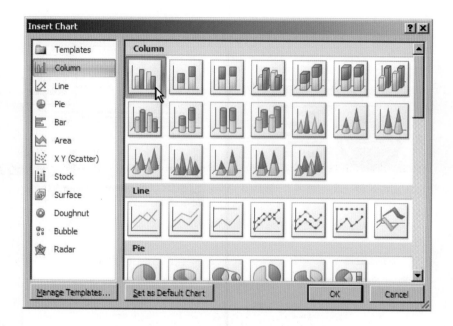

Figure 3.34

 Click **OK**.

Oh dear, it looks awful!

An Excel spreadsheet has opened to help you to produce the chart. Using this is not as bad as it seems.

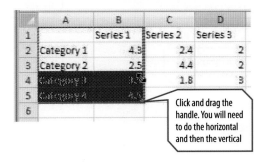

Figure 3.35

99 In the right-hand window (Excel spreadsheet) adjust the data range by dragging the blue handle at the bottom right-hand corner of the selected area; see Figure 3.36.

	A	B	C	D
1		Series 1	Series 2	Series 3
2	Category 1	4.3	2.4	2
3	Category 2	2.5	4.4	2
4	Category 3		1.8	3
5	Category 4			
6				

Click and drag the handle. You will need to do the horizontal and then the vertical

Figure 3.36

Notice the changes made in the chart area in the left-hand window.

As well as changing the number of categories (the number of bars) you can also change the name that will appear below them:

100 Click in cell **A2**, 'Category 1', and type in 'Mentored Pupils'.

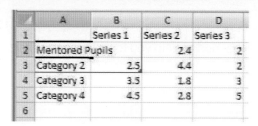

	A	B	C	D
1		Series 1	Series 2	Series 3
2	Mentored Pupils		2.4	2
3	Category 2	2.5	4.4	2
4	Category 3	3.5	1.8	3
5	Category 4	4.5	2.8	5
6				

Figure 3.37

 Change Category 2 to 'Mentors'.

When you click away from the selected area, notice that the chart is updated with the new names.

 Type in the values for number of pupils from the table.

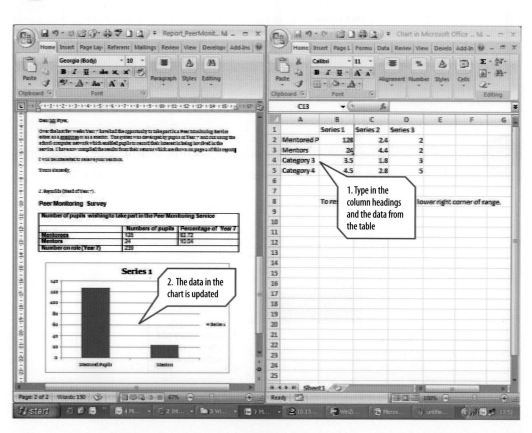

Figure 3.38

82

In the Excel half of your screen click the **Office** button and then select **Save As**:

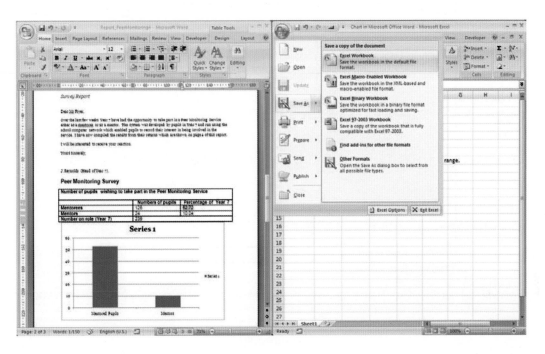

Figure 3.39

 Select **Excel Workbook**.

Save the Excel file in your Report folder; see Figure 3.40.

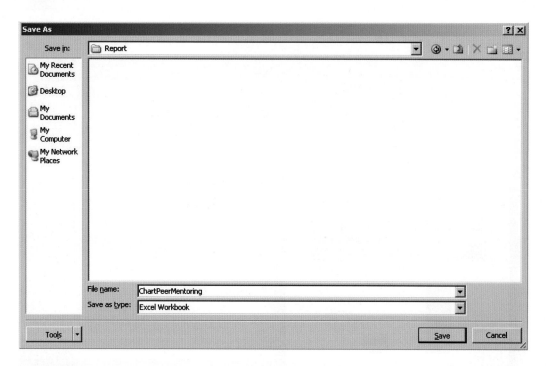

Figure 3.40

 Close the Excel spreadsheet.

 Resize the chart if necessary so that it fits on the same page as the table.

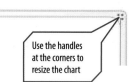

Use the handles at the corners to resize the chart

Figure 3.41

Click on the **Chart Tools Layout** tab.

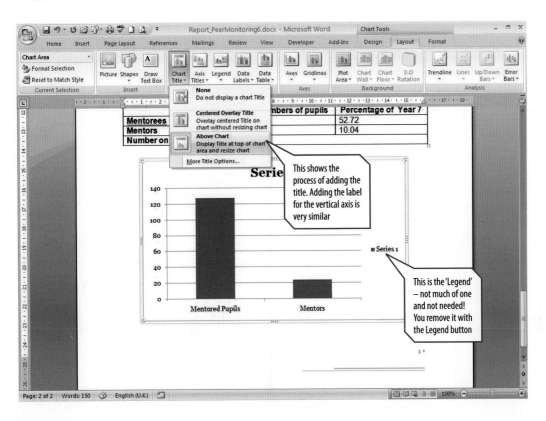

Figure 3.42

Use the buttons to add a title for the chart and label for the vertical axis. Use the **Legend** button to remove the 'Series 1' legend on the right of the chart.

Double click the title, which will probably just have 'Series 1' written in it, delete the text and type in 'Mentoring'.

Replace the text in the label for the vertical axis by clicking on **Axis Titles** and typing 'Number of pupils'.

Have a look at the finished report by clicking on the **View** tab and selecting **Full Screen Reading**.

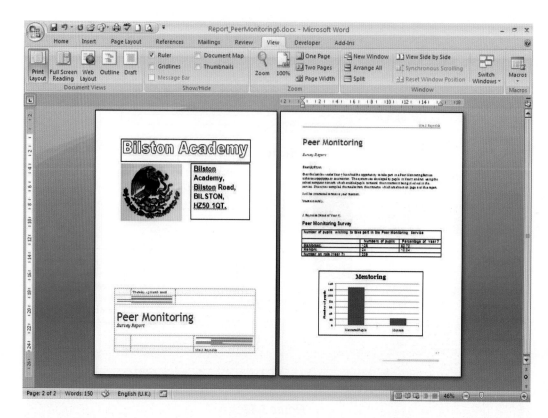

Figure 3.43

 Save your work as **Report_PeerMonitoring8**.

 That's it!

More hyperlinks!

Would hyperlinks improve the use of this report? If the report was sent to Mr Fryer's computer then hyperlinks could be used.

Can you add a hyperlink to the report so that Mr Fryer could also see the form?

CHECKPOINT

Check that you know how to:

> Work methodically and place related files in a folder.

> Change and re-use a pre-formed template.

> Add WordArt to a document.

> Add and format a table.

> Use a formula.

> Add a chart to a document.

> Format a chart so that it displays data from the table and has appropriate labels and title.

ASSESSMENT POINT

Now let's assess the work. Look back at the table at the beginning of this section (**Target point**) and decide on which of the statements you can answer 'Yes' to.

Did you do as well as you expected? Could you improve your work? Use Word to write a comment to show what you could do to improve your work and remember this when starting your next ICT project.

GET AHEAD

The Project is next and you ought to prepare for it because none of the help that you have had in the Tasks will be available. The skills that you will need in the Project are similar to what you have been doing, but without the pictures and written support.

To do well in the Project you need to look back at Tasks 1, 2 and 3, to make sure you can remember the techniques that were demonstrated in them and that you understand why they are used.

Good luck!

TASK BRIEF

You have email!

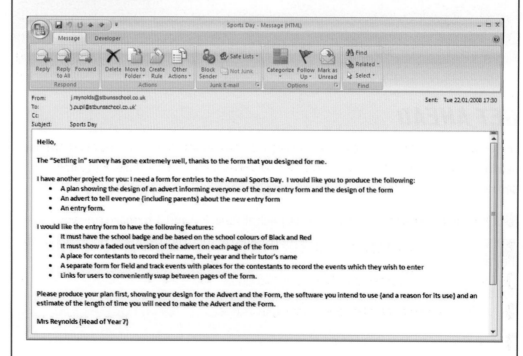

Sports Day - Message (HTML)

Message | Developer

Reply | Reply to All | Forward | Delete | Move to Folder | Create Rule | Other Actions | Block Sender | Not Junk | Safe Lists | Categorize | Follow Up | Mark as Unread | Find | Related | Select

Respond | Actions | Junk E-mail | Options | Find

From: j.reynolds@stbunssschool.co.uk   Sent: Tue 22/01/2008 17:30
To: ').pupil@stbunssschool.co.uk'
Cc:
Subject: Sports Day

Hello,

The "Settling in" survey has gone extremely well, thanks to the form that you designed for me.

I have another project for you: I need a form for entries to the Annual Sports Day. I would like you to produce the following:
- A plan showing the design of an advert informing everyone of the new entry form and the design of the form
- An advert to tell everyone (including parents) about the new entry form
- An entry form.

I would like the entry form to have the following features:
- It must have the school badge and be based on the school colours of Black and Red
- It must show a faded out version of the advert on each page of the form
- A place for contestants to record their name, their year and their tutor's name
- A separate form for field and track events with places for the contestants to record the events which they wish to enter
- Links for users to conveniently swap between pages of the form.

Please produce your plan first, showing your design for the Advert and the Form, the software you intend to use (and a reason for its use) and an estimate of the length of time you will need to make the Advert and the Form.

Mrs Reynolds (Head of Year 7)

Figure Project.1

Over to you!

Brief interlude (and some explanation)

The Introduction and three Tasks should have prepared you for this challenge. We are not expecting you to do anything new, just to apply the knowledge and skills that you have built over the past few weeks to solve a problem.

The problem posed by the Project is very similar to what you have been doing but, as you are in complete control of the way you tackle it, you will be showing 'Capability'. Once you have completed your Project, you should be able to assess your current National Curriculum level.

SOME TIPS

➤ Don't try to do something fancy to impress your teacher. You may be lucky or, more likely, you will spend ages on a technical problem and not finish the Project.

➤ Make sure that your Project does everything in the specification.

➤ Your Project should show that you have considered the audience's needs, for example the type of font used, the Content Controls used. Don't just design your Project to please yourself.

➤ Test your Project (before telling your teacher that you have finished)!

Well, that's enough advice; let's get on with the Project.

To meet this project brief you need to complete Steps 2 and 3, but that is only one part of the process that you would need to go through if you were designing this advert and form for a real Head of Year. The information below shows you how you could go about tackling the other steps in the process. Use the target points to decide how and which of the other steps you want to tackle.

The Functional Skills listed below show you the skills you will be demonstrating in your work – but remember you have to know *why* you have chosen to demonstrate them in a particular way and how your choices match your audience and purpose for the documents.

➤ Planning your documents.

➤ Using suitable software for your advert and form.

➤ Saving your documents with suitable filenames.

➤ Using a suitable template and document layout.

➤ Editing text with suitable fonts and styles.

➤ Inserting and editing images.

➤ Testing and reviewing your documents.

RESURCES

Name of resource	Type of resource	Use
Asset_1	Picture file	To produce the advert
Asset_2	Picture file	To produce the advert
Asset_3	Picture file	To produce the advert
Asset_4	Word file	Information for the advert
Asset_5	Word file	Information for the form
Asset_6	Picture file	Image of the school badge

ADVICE

Work in the following order:

Produce a plan for the advert and the form. Use plain paper and do the following:

> Re-read the email and write down what you need to do as a list.

> Make a pencil and paper drawing of the layout of the advert.

> Make a pencil and paper drawing of the layout of the form. You will use the advert as a template for the form, but you will also need to show where the title and text boxes to hold the information and content controls are going to be placed. Check with the email from Mrs Reynolds for the type of controls you need.

> Write on your paper the software that you are going to use and give a reason for your choice.

> Write on your paper an estimate of how long you will need to make the advert and form.

Make the advert:

> Make a suitable title.

> Use four 'Assets' (Assets 1, 2, 3 and 6) to make an interesting advert.

> Add a text box to hold written information from Asset_4.

> Use the arrangement tools to make the title and all of the information visible.

Make the form:

> Save the advert as a template.

> Save the template with a new filename as a start to making the form.

> Press the **Blank Page** button (**Insert** tab, **Pages** group) twice to make a total of three pages (or repeatedly press **Enter**).

> Copy the image used for the background to each of the forms. You could use the same image for all three pages or you could use different images on each page. The images should not distract from the view of the form.

> Insert content controls (check with your plan for the type and number that you need).

 Check that you have done everything that has been asked.

Test your solution:

> Make a copy of the table and its headings from Task 3.

> Think of the different *tests* that should be done and write these down in the *first* column.

> Think about *how* you can do the tests and write this in the *second* column.

> Think about what a *successful* result will be; this goes in the *third* column.

> Now carry out your tests and complete the last two columns.

> If there are any faults, you will know because the actual and expected results will not match.

> You should try to put right the faults you find, and then test again.

6 Evaluation:

➤ Compare your solution with the email.

➤ Fill in a copy of this table:

Feature	1 (worst)	2	3	4	5 (best)
How well it works					
What it looks like					
How well it suits the audience					
How well it solves Mrs Reynolds' problem					

Shade in to show how well you think you have done for each feature.

➤ Now write three sentences about how you have done and three sentences about how you could improve.

7 Check your work against the table on page 93. This will give you some idea of the National Curriculum level for your work on this Project (ICT has many other sections, so this is just a guide to how you are getting on).

8 Submit your work. You should make sure that you have the following:

➤ Your plans for the advert, form and software/time taken.

➤ The advert.

➤ The form.

➤ The test plan table.

➤ Your evaluation.

Elements of capability	Level 3	Level 4	Level 5	Level 6
PLANNING	You have produced a basic plan	You cannot be awarded levels for this activity because I gave you the sequence for working. You have now had experience of planning and in a future project a proper assessment can be made		
ORGANISING	You have used save	You have saved a file in a new folder	You have saved the file as a Word file	
	You have used a folder for files	You have set up a new folder for the files in this Project		
	You have used textboxes	You have rearranged the page	You have used assets in the advert and in the form	
	You have inserted a control	You have added an item to the combo box		
		You have used a template	You have added items to the template	
INFORMATION Combining and refining	You have added an image to the advert or form	You have added information and an image	You have arranged an advert or form to make it suitable for its intended audience	You have integrated a badge, controls and information into the form
	You have used a hyperlink	You have added a hyperlink	You have added a hyperlink and a bookmark	
PRESENTING INFORMATION	You have produced an advert	Your advert is made from image(s) and text	Your advert and form are suitable for their intended audience	
	You have taken care not to obscure text when positioning the image	You have used formatting to distinguish the title from other text	You have used Format Paintbrush to change the formatting in a group of text boxes	
	You have changed the size and position of an image following advice	You have changed the size of images to make the advert and form more suitable for their intended audience	You have independently altered formatting (text, text boxes, style of image) to suit the intended audience	You have taken care to design the advert and form to suit both pupils and parents
			You have independently developed at least two hyperlinks to aid in the navigation of the form	

(Continued.)

TARGET POINT

Have a look at the following statements before you start your project so you know what you are aiming for.

Elements of capability	Level 3	Level 4	Level 5	Level 6
REVIEWING TESTING EVALUATING		You have performed a basic test	You have performed a test to examine whether the combo box operates correctly and the rich text box accepts data	You have designed and run a test on the rich text box to find whether there are limitations on the data entered
	You have checked for correct functioning of the hyperlink	You have checked that the hyperlink causes a move to the correct bookmark		
	You have carried out a basic evaluation	You have evaluated the product you have made against the specification in the email	You have evaluated whether the advert OR form is suitable for the intended audience	

ASSESSMENT POINT

Now let's assess the work. Look at the table above (**Target point**) and decide on which of the statements you can answer 'Yes' to.

Did you do as well as you expected? Could you improve your work? Use Word to write a comment to show what you could do to improve your work and remember this when starting your next ICT project.

INDEX

Addresses, formatting 69–70
Advert and form project 88–94
  about the project 88–9
  advice 90–2
  resources 90
Aspect ratio, locking 51
Author control 72
Axis Titles 85

Bold fonts 44
Bookmarks 54–6

Chart, formatting 80–6
  Axis Titles 85
  Chart Tools Layout 85
  Clustered Column style 80
  Excel spreadsheet 81–4
  Legend button 85
Check Box control 33–6, 37
Content Control
  Properties box 26–32
Control boxes
  box 1 – name 22–4
  box 2 – date 25–6
  box 3 – best subject 27–9
  box 4 – subjects needing
    help 30
  box 5 – help finding way
    around 30
  box 6 – any problems 31
  box 7 – picture 32–3
  box 8 – peer monitoring 33–6
Controls, inserting 19–20
Copy and paste 18–19

Cover Page 49–53
  contents for 50
  icon for 49
  templates 49

Date 25–6
  Date Picker button 25–6
  formatting 70–2
  styles available 71
Design Mode 63
Developer tab 22, 63
Document Views 62
Drop-Down Lists 27–9

Excel spreadsheet 81–4
Excel Workbook 83–4

Folders, new 13
Fonts
  Bold 44
  dialogue box 45
  size 44
Form creation 10–39
  about form creation 12
  inserting controls 19–20
  organising for saving 13
  planning 14
  setting tabs 20–1
  Task 1 brief 10
  titles 17–19
  see also Control boxes
Formatting 40–57
  Bold 44
  font size 44

highlighting 44
lower/upper case 45
organising for 42–3
picture size 51
Picture Styles group 52
Shape Fill 52
Shape Outline 52
Shapes icon 45
Size and rotate pane 51
testing 56
Text Wrapping 46, 51–2
see also Cover Page;
  Hyperlinks
Formatting the report
  the address 69–70
  Author control 72
  the date 70–2
  the document title 72
  the graph (or chart) 80–6
  the heading 66–8
  the letter 72–3
  Subtitle control 72
  the table 73–9
  WordArt 66–8
Full Screen Reading
  button 79, 86

Graph, formatting 80–6
  see also Chart, Formatting

Highlighting 44
Hotspots 54
Hyperlinks 54–6
  Bookmarks 54–6

Edit Hyperlink 55
hotspots 54
with report production 86
Shape Styles 55

Insert Picture dialogue box 64–5
Insertion point cursor 17

Legacy Toolbox 34
Legend button 85
Letters, formatting 72–3
Lower/upper case 45

Microsoft Office Security
Options box 43

New Style button 23–4

Organising
for formatting 42–3
for saving 13

Picture Content control 32–3, 37
disappearance of 36
testing 47–8
Pictures
Insert Picture 47
Picture Styles group 52
size 51
Planning documents 14
Printing files 9
Print Preview 9
Project see Advert and form
project
Proofing section 7
Properties
Content Control
Properties box 26–32
dialogue box 35–6

Quick Access toolbar 12

Redo button 12
Report production 58–87
organising for 60–1
see also Formatting the
report; Templates
Review tab 7
Rich Text control 22–3, 31
Rows & Columns group 78
Ruler, using 18

Saving files 7–9, 13
choices for 8
Save As 7–9, 38
Shapes
button 17–18
icon 45
Shape Fill 52
Shape Outline, No Outline 52
Shape Styles 55
Show Developer tab 21
Size and rotate pane 51
Spelling and Grammar check 7
Split Cells 76–7
Starting
for formatting 42–3
Word 5
Subtitle control 72

Tables, formatting 73–9
formula button/
dialogue box 77–8
Rows & Columns group 78
Split Cells 76–7
Table Tools 76–7
Tabs
new tabs 34
setting 20–1
tab toolbox 20
Task briefs

Task 1: form creation 10
Task 2: formatting 40–57
Task 3: report production 58
advert and form project 88
Templates
choosing 61–2
for Cover Page 49
layout 62–86
see also Formatting the
report
Testing
formatting 56
Picture Content control 47–8
Task 1 testing 38
Text Box 65–6
Text Wrapping 46, 51–2
Titles 17–19

Undo button 12

View tab
Document Views 62
for templates 62–3

Watermarks 15–16
Word 2007
about Word 4–5
main tools 7
Proofing section 7
Review tab 7
screen features 6
starting 5
tabs and ribbons 6
Word Macro-Enabled
Document box 38, 48
Word Options box 21
WordArt 66–8